WE ARE ONE
VILLAGE

Nikki Lovell

WE ARE ONE VILLAGE

The inspiring true story of an African community's impact on a young Australian girl

ALLEN&UNWIN
SYDNEY·MELBOURNE·AUCKLAND·LONDON

First published in 2012
Copyright © Nikki Lovell 2012

Author's note: All of the events and people in this book are real; however, some names have been changed to protect privacy.

All rights reserved. No part of this book may be reproduced or transmitted in any form or by any means, electronic or mechanical, including photocopying, recording or by any information storage and retrieval system, without prior permission in writing from the publisher. The Australian *Copyright Act 1968* (the Act) allows a maximum of one chapter or 10 per cent of this book, whichever is the greater, to be photocopied by any educational institution for its educational purposes provided that the educational institution (or body that administers it) has given a remuneration notice to Copyright Agency Limited (CAL) under the Act.

Allen & Unwin
Sydney, Melbourne, Auckland, London
83 Alexander Street
Crows Nest NSW 2065
Australia
Phone: (61 2) 8425 0100
Fax: (61 2) 9906 2218
Email: info@allenandunwin.com
Web: www.allenandunwin.com

Cataloguing-in-Publication details are available
from the National Library of Australia
www.trove.nla.gov.au

ISBN 978 1 74237 836 7

Set in 13/17.5 pt Granjon by Post Pre-press Group, Australia
Printed and bound in Australia by the SOS Print + Media Group.

10 9 8 7 6 5 4 3

The paper in this book is FSC® certified. FSC® promotes environmentally responsible, socially beneficial and economically viable management of the world's forests.

One who sees something good must narrate it.
Ugandan proverb

Contents

1 Women to Remember   1
2 Saying Goodbye   19
3 The North Star   35
4 A Magical Place   55
5 Bad News   75
6 A Kiss and a Kill   91
7 Lessons on Love   109
8 My Brother Josh   127
9 How We Cope   151
10 The Hardest Thing   171
11 The Phone Call   191
12 Catch 22   207
13 One Village   227

Acknowledgements   237
About One Village   239

1
Women to Remember

NAMWENDWA, UGANDA, 1 May 2005

I will always remember Harriet squeezing my hand, her big brown eyes locking with mine. My heart was beating uncontrollably, loud and heavy. I was convinced I could hear it echoing around the room, draining out the doctor's words.

A week earlier Harriet had approached me with four other girls and asked me to take them to be tested at a HIV clinic. All five girls were students in Senior 3 (which is equivalent to about Year 10 in Australia) and I was one of the health teachers at St Peter's Secondary School. I guess teaching health made me seem like the ideal candidate to take them to be tested. Health was never taught as a subject before we had arrived in the village earlier in the year. This made me wonder whether it was hearing about HIV in class that had prompted the girls to be tested, or if I was just the first person they felt comfortable asking about it. I didn't think it appropriate to ask, but of course I agreed and the plan was made.

We agreed to meet at 7 a.m. at the trading centre in Namwendwa sub-county. Namwendwa was also the name of the village where I lived and worked. Four villages made up the sub-county and the trading centre was the hub where they all met. Over 55 000 people lived within the sub-county, which was about 180 kilometres west of the Kenyan border and 130 kilometres north of Uganda's capital, Kampala.

The night before, I was so nervous I didn't sleep. I was eighteen and any real knowledge I had of HIV had only been recently acquired. The girls I would be taking on the bus to the medical centre in the nearby town of Kamuli were even younger than me—they were probably about sixteen, but in Uganda everyone is pretty vague about ages. No-one celebrates birthdays. Initially I assumed this was because of monetary restraints, but later I came to realise that significance was instead placed on other life milestones, such as boys reaching manhood.

I imagined that the girls too had laid awake the previous night, staring at the ceiling. What would we do if they tested positive? Jane, who was British and a few years older than me, was also teaching health at the school and I had thought that she would be more suitable to take the girls. I'd tried to convince her of this, and we ended up flipping a coin over it.

The coin had landed all the responsibility on me. Whatever the tests showed, I would have to be there for the girls, but I had no idea how I would do that.

As I walked to the trading centre, people were waking and beginning their daily chores. Women were sitting in front of their mud huts, charcoal stoves alight and tea boiling. '*Jambo!*' (hello) they called out to me, smiling and waving.

Giggling children raced past me. The jerry cans they were carrying swung wildly about, clinking into each other as the children bounced along on their way to get water. I pictured the borehole buzzing with activity. It was roughly 2 kilometres from my home to the trading centre and I always enjoyed the walk. It was a dusty red road, with lush greenery overflowing onto it, and this particular morning the sky was a magnificent baby blue. Walking down that road the sky always looked like it enclosed the village, as though we were in a snow globe, except without the snow. Somehow, when I was in Namwendwa, it felt like there was nowhere else in the world. For me this was a relaxing and peaceful thought, but I couldn't help wondering if sometimes the place just seemed so beautiful because at any moment I could walk away. For most people in Namwendwa, there literally was nowhere else. As such thoughts began cluttering my mind, the walk became less enjoyable.

As I came nearer to the trading centre, the trees were replaced with little stalls—people selling a few tomatoes or a pineapple. Here the red road was littered with rubbish—fluttering bits of paper and scraps, the occasional empty soda bottle. In the heart of the village, where I lived, it was still magical and clean—people could not afford to buy anything that would produce rubbish. But the trading centre, being the hub of four villages, was a little bit different—around it were a few small shops and there were no bins anywhere. Some people burnt their rubbish, but bits and pieces always seemed to escape the flames and other things simply refused to be destroyed. Most people didn't bother with burning; they threw their rubbish straight on the ground.

A *matatu* (a little bus, but really what we would call a 'people mover' with benches for seats, and an aisle down the side which would later be filled with fold-down seats) was waiting by the roundabout of the trading centre. The five girls were gathered around it. My negative thoughts about the litter were replaced by nervousness, but I forced myself to smile as I approached the girls and greeted them.

The girls were quiet. I was used to seeing them in school uniform, so it was strange to see them in casual clothes. They all wore long skirts, with colourful shirts that clashed. Harriet stood out. Her high-waisted denim skirt was fitted, whereas women in the village generally wore looser clothing.

We all clambered onto the *matatu*, not really knowing what to say to each other. The conductor was lying across the back row of seats. I suspected that he had been asleep, but he woke as we entered. He clambered over the seats to get to the front, gesturing for us to go to the back. We were the only ones in the *matatu* and it would not leave until it was completely full. It was licensed to carry fourteen passengers but, to a *matatu* driver, full meant at least twenty people—plus probably a few chickens by your feet, maybe a goat with its legs tied, and a whole heap of luggage on the roof.

This morning it took two hours for the little bus to fill, as not many people were travelling from Namwendwa to Kamuli. Most people lived off their land and had no reason or excess funds for travel, even though the fare for this particular journey was only 1000 shillings (around 60 cents). By the time we were preparing to leave, it was impossible for anyone else to enter through the sliding door at the side—every possible space had been filled, with six or seven people crammed onto each row of seats and fold-downs where there had earlier been an aisle.

Just as the engine began to splutter into life, an elderly man appeared by my window. The *matatu* conductor, who was standing (or more accurately being held upright by confinement) had spotted the man and began yelling in Lusoga (the local language). At first I thought he was rebuking the man, demanding that he move out of the way. But as those outside who had been watching all this began to encircle the old man, I realised that quite the opposite was happening. The conductor didn't want him moved away—he wanted him inside the bus!

The next burst of yelling from the conductor was aimed at me, and I didn't need to speak Lusoga to know he wanted me to slide the window open. This was difficult to do as dust from the road had wedged it tightly shut. I used all my weight to push against the window, silently begging for it to give way. Finally, the window creaked open and the elderly man was lifted up by the people outside so he could slide in through the small open space. His head ended up on the lap of one of the girls; his body was curled up to fit in a lying position across the others and his feet landed up on me. With the addition of the elderly man, the conductor was finally satisfied. I promptly pulled the window shut again and, with the *matatu* almost overflowing with limbs, we started to rattle on our way.

During all this waiting the girls had said very little. I hadn't contributed much to the conversation either. I had wanted to say something, but under the circumstances everything I thought of seemed pathetic. So I was happy when we raced along and it was too loud and physically awkward to say anything. I stared out the window and waved as we passed excited children screaming out, '*Munzungu, munzungu!*'(White person, white person). Being white made me a celebrity but I didn't particularly like being an attraction because of my skin colour. Actually, I didn't like it at all.

Although it was still quite early, the sun's heat was already intense, especially inside the *matatu*. I could feel the sweat building underneath me on my seat and between my shoulder and Harriet's, who was squashed up next to me. I glanced down at the man's feet, still nestled in my lap, and my eyes widened as I saw drops of sweat fall in slow motion from his heels and plop onto my skirt. Ugh! I forced my attention back out the window.

Kamuli was only 16 kilometres from Namwendwa so the trip didn't take long—once we actually got going, that is. Nevertheless, I was grateful when we arrived and I could step out into open space. I peeled my skirt and shirt loose from my body; everything was stuck with sweat, even my hair was wet and clinging to my face.

The girls and I hadn't been standing there a minute before we were approached by *buda-buda* men (men on motorbikes or pedalling bicycles with a dinky seat), wanting to take us to where we were going. I really felt like walking after our claustrophobic experience on the *matatu* but, as the girls shuffled anxiously around me, it was obvious that getting there as fast as possible was the priority.

I negotiated for the best price, but paused before hopping on the back of my bike. Ideally I would have liked to have had one leg on each side, so as to be well balanced, but my skirt was long and hoisting it up would have attracted unwanted attention. So side-saddling it was, for all of us. We travelled two girls per bike, with no helmets, and I enjoyed the sensation of the wind sweeping through my hair. The girls looked so graceful sitting sideways, while I somehow wobbled about, even though I was squashed into position between the driver and one of my companions.

The medical clinic was a simple white building. I had expected it to be frantic inside, but instead it seemed to be abandoned. The girls and I sat on a bench outside and waited for someone to appear. Silence. Then Harriet moved closer to me. I noticed that her body was trembling.

'My father died of AIDS,' she whispered, her eyes focused on the ground.

She was about to say something else and then stopped herself. I knew what she was thinking: that if he had died from AIDS, then surely she had HIV.

Moments passed. Then she looked at me, just briefly, before saying: 'Who would look after my brothers and sisters?'

I reached over to her, taking her hand from her lap, and holding it firmly in my own hand. Our hands sat interlocked on the bench between us. I didn't say anything; I couldn't.

It seemed like forever before a Ugandan doctor in a white coat emerged from the white building. I jumped up, and moved toward him. I greeted him and told him that the girls were here to be HIV tested.

The man shook his head, 'No testing today,' he replied. 'Come back tomorrow.'

My blood started to sizzle and I began rambling nervously, explaining how the girls had already waited too long and pleading for him to give us just a few moments of his time. But the man looked at me blankly and shook his head. I felt overwhelmed by disappointment and despair as the doctor turned back to the door.

'Well, is there somewhere else we can go?' I blurted out. He was losing his patience with me now; he turned quickly and told me that there was another clinic, but that he didn't know the name of it. He gave me vague directions and then disappeared.

I did my best to look confident as I walked back to the girls. Their faces turned to me in anticipation. I told them there was a better clinic, and that we should go there instead. As we walked away from the clinic I was trying very hard to act as if I was totally in control of the situation. I was confused by the directions the doctor had given, but I kept walking anyway. After half an hour, we were completely lost. I was sweating again, and my head pounded from dehydration. *Shit!* The girls had depended on me and I was proving useless. I was looking around for any indication of where we might be when a *buda-buda* man bobbed up next to us.

'*Munzungu, munzungu*, I take you.'

I asked him if he knew of another medical clinic. He nodded. I didn't entirely believe him, but at that stage I was desperate. So we waited while he went to find two more drivers. True to his word, he returned with two other *buda-buda* men, and soon we were on our way.

The other clinic was a brick building, with two doors. One of the doors was open, which was a nice change after the white building that had rejected us. We entered it rather tentatively and were immediately hit by the distinctive smell of urine, which hung in the air. The room was empty except for five metal beds, two of which were broken. None of the beds were occupied. The girls and I stood awkwardly among the beds before a nurse entered and welcomed us. I explained our purpose and she smiled and gestured to a bench outside. So we sat on yet another bench and waited.

Fortunately a local doctor soon appeared. He greeted us with a smile and indicated that we should follow him into a small room. I was grateful that the urine smell was not present in this little room and, instead of beds, there was a wooden desk, which the kind doctor promptly sat behind. He motioned for us to sit down as well, which seemed odd to me given there were six of us and only one chair. The girls told me to sit down and I reluctantly did so. The doctor explained that he would need to speak first with each girl before they were tested and ask a series of questions by way of pre-counselling. He took down all the girls' names and then directed us back outside to the waiting bench. Soon after we sat down, he came outside and glanced down at his little notebook.

'Harriet?' he read out.

She stood quickly, and then turned to me expectantly. I followed her back into the room and this time I insisted that she take the seat. I stood toward the back corner of the room. The doctor's questions were extremely personal, and I felt that I was invading Harriet's privacy. When she hesitated in answering, I wondered whether I should leave the room. There wasn't an opportunity to ask her though, so I continued to stand silently in the corner. After the questions, it was time for the HIV test. I watched as the doctor took a needle and Harriet held out her arm, but as he edged closer to her, I looked away. When I turned back again, she was standing up and I noticed a spot of blood on her arm—no cotton ball nicely stuck on here.

The doctor followed her out of the room and called in the next girl. I stayed in the room, looking awkwardly about. In the end, I stayed with each of the girls during their pre-counselling and testing. That was the easy bit. The hard part was then trying to distract them for an hour and a half while we waited for their results; without a doubt that was the most difficult wait, and the minutes crept by painfully slowly.

The girls were quiet, although I had no doubt that their minds were filled with a commotion of loud thoughts. We wandered across to some nearby market stalls and I bought us *chapattis* and *menvu* (small bananas). I also bought the girls sodas for a treat, and a bottle of water for myself, which was warm but nonetheless refreshing after the long morning.

Back at the clinic we sat waiting once more. The bench was starting to feel all too familiar. But finally the doctor reappeared and announced that he had the results.

Harriet was called into his office first. Once again she turned to me, and again I followed in after her. Interestingly, where there had previously been only one wooden chair, there were now two, so Harriet and I both took a seat. The doctor sat down too, behind his little desk, and the young girl's eyes began to dart around the room in fear. As before, she took my hand in hers.

Time seemed to be passing interminably slowly. My heart could not have beaten any faster. When the doctor spoke at last, his voice sounded like a blur. I could hardly make out what he was saying. Except for one word—'negative'.

Harriet and I both burst into tears. The relief was overwhelming.

The other girls were happy to receive their test results on their own. From the chatter that followed as we walked out of the clinic, I could tell it had been good news all around. I wasn't foolish enough to trust my sense of directions (or lack thereof) to guide us back to the *matatu* station, so it was *buda-budas*, slow pottering and wind through my hair once more. The only difference was the laughter of the girls, which seemed to vibrate all around me.

Back at Namwendwa trading centre, I hugged the girls goodbye in turn. Harriet was last.

'Thank you,' she said softly, her eyes still wet with relief.

I smiled at her reassuringly and said that I would see her at school tomorrow. She turned and followed the other girls back down the dusty red road.

I started slowly in the same direction, but then I detoured, deciding that I would visit my friend Florence. When I got close to her house she saw me coming and she raced onto the road. 'Niiikkkkkkkkkiiiiiiiiiiii!' she literally squealed with joy as she wrapped me in a long hug.

Then she took my hand in hers and led me up to her home. I waited just outside while she raced into the house and then reappeared with two handmade wooden chairs. Most women in the village sat on coloured woven mats, while chairs were normally reserved for men. But that was a practice Florence never followed. We always sat outside her home, although I had been inside once before. She was better off than most in the community: where most people had thatched huts, her home was brick and had a solid roof. It was still a single room though, which she shared with her husband and children. I think she had seven, but I struggled to remember their names. They all shared the same few outfits, so I was often confused about who was who.

Florence—whom we had met at a community meeting—was able to afford such a home because she had built an infants school in her backyard. I call it a school because that's what it was, but perhaps that creates a false impression of its structure. Its single classroom was made of bamboo and sat behind Florence's home. Years earlier she had had the ingenious idea of creating a combined pre-school and early years primary school. There was already a primary school in the village, which was government-run and essentially free for students to attend. This was one of the schools where I taught and so I knew firsthand that its classrooms had no resources and it was seriously overcrowded. The children had to sit squashed on the dirt floor because there were over 70 kids in each class. Parents obviously wanted better facilities for their children, but there was no other option. One problem was that the only people earning an income in the village were the teachers and those who worked in the trading centre. Florence, a trained teacher herself, thought that if she could set up her own school and charge a small fee for students to attend, she could both earn an income to support her large family and provide a service for the community. The idea had worked exactly as she planned—and Florence had also been able to employ three other teachers. Class sizes were small, with some lessons taught inside the bamboo building and others taught outside.

I loved watching Florence teach. She was always very creative and fun with the kids. She taught the alphabet by singing with them, and they learned the meaning of words by drawing pictures.

As we sat outside that afternoon she clasped her hands together and exclaimed, 'Madam Nik! How are you?'

I was exhausted, so I let Florence do the talking. She became excited, almost bouncing out of her chair as she told me of her plans for developing her school. She never talked about dreams—only plans. A few of her children gathered around us, the youngest one tugging at her skirt while staring at me. Florence picked up the little boy and bobbed him up and down. Goggle-eyed, his focus remained on me. I gave him a big smile.

'*Jambo!*'

This was too much for him. His little head swung around to face his mother, screaming and crying both at once. The poor boy was terrified. As I stood up to leave, Florence passed the boy into the waiting arms of one of the older children, who carried him inside. To reassure me, my friend asked that I stay.

But I was tired and ready to go home. Florence took my hand and walked me back out to the road. As I hugged her goodbye, I noticed that there was construction taking place next to her house. I was surprised I hadn't noticed it before. The sound of the workers suddenly seemed very loud and unpleasant. I asked Florence what was going on and she told me that they were building a phone tower. Then she hugged me again, and turned back to her home.

A phone tower? In a rural village where there was no electricity and no running water, where people lived in mud huts and school was a luxury? I was shocked. Not pleased, or dismayed, just shocked.

As I entered my red-road, lush-greenery and blue-sky world, I thought that communication must be one of the most valuable things to have. I never realised at the time how true that would prove.

At home, I found Jane squatting outside beside the charcoal stove. We shared a home and did most activities together. We also shared the novelty of being the only white women in the village.

I snuck up on her, but instead of Jane being surprised it was our dinner that seemed startled. There was a pot on the stove with a plate resting on top as a makeshift lid. As I spoke, the plate suddenly came alive and began wobbling frantically.

Jane quickly spun her head around in my direction, said hello, and then grabbed a piece of cloth and removed the plate. I dashed inside and reappeared with a wooden chair. I made myself comfortable, but then thought better of it and stood up again, asking how I could help.

Jane instructed me to get some plates and cutlery. These were stored neatly in the yellow basin. I also grabbed the purple woven mat and returned outside. I laid the mat on the grass and took the plates and cutlery to the now pot-less stove. Jane was draining the beans by the side of the house. We served up but just as we settled back on the mat to eat,

Robert, who lived nearby, wandered over and greeted us. He was tall and sturdy but I guessed he was only about sixteen. His face looked like the moon when he smiled—round and gentle.

When I asked how he was, his large feet shuffled in the dirt and his face tilted toward our stove. The sky had just started to darken and the coals glowed magnificently. I nodded toward the coals and offered for Robert to take them. His smile widened. He was holding his family's stove (a small metal stand, which the coals would rest on while a pot would be balanced on top), and he moved toward the coals and quickly plucked them up. He thanked us in his soft voice. My eyes followed him home. He was wearing the same clothes that he wore every day—torn three-quarter length pants and a ripped white T-shirt with faded blurs of colour where a logo had once lived.

Without any further ado, I tucked into dinner—the beans and rice were delicious. I also asked Jane how school had been today.

'Well,' she began, swallowing a large forkful, 'quite eventful, actually!'

She went on to explain all that I had missed—a lot can happen in a day. We talked, and laughed, and ate. By the time I had finished I was so full that I had to lie down on the mat. Jane told me there was still more left but I couldn't eat another bite. I grasped at my stomach, which now contained a bean and rice baby. We had no way to keep food cold or stored, which meant that we often over-ate. However, the previous few nights we had taken the leftovers to our neighbours. I was just about to suggest this when young Victoria and her even younger sister, Mirimu, skipped over. I sat up and Victoria nestled in my lap. She pulled my hair free from its ponytail and twisted it around her fingers. She glanced up at me with her beautiful brown eyes framed by her long dark eyelashes. In Lusoga I asked her about her day. But instead of answering, she smiled shyly and focused on my hair.

Jane placed her plate to the side as Mirimu launched in for a cuddle. Soon other children started to gather on the mat. It was very dark now, and it was difficult to differentiate their faces. I lifted Victoria from my lap, and raced inside to grab the kerosene lamp. I placed it beside the mat but, instead of sitting down again, I reached for Victoria's hand, pulled her up and started singing. The children leaped up in a great burst of giggles. Everyone raced off the grass to a larger patch of dirt. A circle was formed and, with hands tightly clasped together, we skipped around singing. I still didn't know all the words, but I understood when it was time to squat down, or jump up, or when we all ran together into the centre of the circle and threw our hands in the air. It was ridiculously fun.

We played until older siblings of the children came and took the younger ones home for bed. Then Jane and I retired to the mat. We lay down and gazed at the stars. Other than the small glow from our lamp, the village was pitch black and the stars were unbelievable.

Soon my eyelids started to feel heavy but as I stood to go inside to bed, I suddenly remembered the leftover dinner.

Jane and I looked around; but there were no signs that any of our neighbours were still awake. We decided that we should try knocking next door anyway, but first we carried our dirty plates inside and put them in a basin. We then put another basin upside down on top of it, before placing a brick on top as a weight—to rat-proof it. Then I carried the lamp while Jane heaped the leftover beans into the pot with the remaining rice, and we made our way next door.

I was feeling unsure about disturbing our neighbour, but when the dark silhouette answered and we showed him the pot, his white teeth glistened out from a big smile. '*Webale, webaleino.*' (Thank you, thank you).

By the time I finally crawled into bed and tucked my mozzie net carefully into the mattress, I was exhausted. I could hear the rats in the other room, pushing against the basins and knocking against the unbalanced little table. Soon they would be in our room, scurrying about under our beds, but I was too tired to care.

'*Sula burungi* (goodnight), *Kawooda*,' Jane called out.

Kawooda was my village name. It was the name given to the youngest girl when twins were born.

'*Sula burungi, Babida.*'

The night before I had been restless and full of self-doubt, but now I felt peaceful. I imagined Harriet would sleep with ease tonight, and I felt happy that maybe I had played a part in that. I dozed off with a full belly and a full heart.

2

Saying Goodbye

ADELAIDE, SOUTH AUSTRALIA, October–December 2004

There were two men in my kitchen and they were stealing my attention. I was sitting at the kitchen table, and they were directly in my line of vision with only the table and kitchen bench between us. I wasn't entirely sure what they were doing there—fixing the fridge maybe? Whatever it was, they were making a lot of noise. They were attractive men, with tanned muscular bodies, but this was not the time to be distracted.

I was studying for my Year 12 exams, or at least attempting to. This was the closing chapter of a significant stage of my life and I felt it warranted a little more attention. But for Mum and Dad this was also a time for endings and beginnings and they had decided to sell the house. In a few months they were moving to Ireland, and Dad was going to work as a doctor in a medical clinic there. Mum had given up her job as a social worker and was going to look after my younger brother, Josh, who was going with them. My older brother, Sam, planned to stay in Adelaide. And I still didn't know what I was going to do.

During school my friends sometimes referred to my family as The Addams Family. We certainly never had a butler, neither my two brothers nor I were named after a day of the week, and I never saw my dad elaborately kiss my mum's arms, but there was always something happening in our house. Every day at school I seemed to have a different story: Josh had flushed his glasses down the toilet; my nanna had temporarily moved in; my dad was living in Antarctica for a year—yes, these things actually happened. I lived in a busy, sometimes crazy family. There was never a dull—or quiet—moment.

As if to prove my point, the men in the kitchen started making a grinding noise. Admittedly I could have been studying in my room, but I liked to have my books and notes spread across the kitchen table. It made me feel more productive even if it was just a scattered mess. Of course it was useless anyway—I couldn't concentrate. I was wondering where Mum was. I needed to complain about our house turning into a workshop. I was feeling a bit sorry for myself and singing the song 'What About Me' in my head—I knew that any chance of memorising my legal studies notes was well and truly gone once that happened. I stood up and the men in the kitchen looked at me.

For a moment I worried that I had actually been singing out loud. No, not possible. If that was the case they would have been staring, not merely looking, and they would have had expressions of disgust—I'm an awful singer. I quickly smiled at the men and then wandered outside, grabbing a book from the kitchen bench on my way. I sat by the pool and opened it. Mum had brought it home for me the night before. It was a good ole Lonely Planet Book called *The Gap Year*.

For as long as I could recall, I had been dreaming of the wild adventures that I would embark on post school. Since I was 15 I had worked in a cafe and then a bakery, saving every dollar I earned. I was very proud that I now had $10 000 in the bank. My only problem was that freedom was looming and I had absolutely no plans. I had heard a saying once that the best way to know oneself was to remove yourself from everything you know. That's what I wanted to do. Although not to discover myself or anything like that. I knew who I was and what I wanted—I wanted a wild adventure.

Whenever I became excited about this prospect, I always thought of Africa. I knew little about the continent, but it fascinated me. I imagined vibrant and diverse landscapes, cultures and people. In my mind I could see various tribes dressed in bright clothes and wearing beaded necklaces. And then such beautiful thoughts would be interrupted by different imagery—of tragedy, of famines, of corrupt governments, of child soldiers. This was the Africa the media had shown me. But I wanted to learn about the place for myself, to truly understand the sad pictures that so often appeared on my TV screen.

The Gap Year had a section that listed opportunities for volunteering in different African countries. As I read it, I realised how lovely it was to be outside. It was a sunny day with just a slight breeze. I couldn't help watching the wind dance through the leaves, which rustled as if the breeze was tickling them. I have always liked how the wind can only be seen through its effect. It reminded me of love—you cannot see love, except in the way it makes your step lighter, or your eyes sparkle, or your smile become goofy even when you are talking about something ordinary like what you'd eaten for breakfast.

The wind swept through my hands and turned a few pages. I remembered that I had been reading and flipped the pages back to find my spot. I was not finding much inspiration in the organisations that occupied each page. Maybe I was sitting too much on my moral high-horse but all the placements seemed tokenistic, like '2 weeks building a classroom with volunteers from all over the world, then a 2 week safari!' I didn't know much about these countries—okay, I didn't really know anything at all—but nevertheless I was pretty sure that the local people could probably construct a building for themselves. I sighed. I didn't want to just feel like I was doing something worthwhile—I actually wanted it *to be worthwhile*! And I had a whole year.

Sometime later Mum found me by the pool. She sat with me and patiently listened to me whinge about the lack of exciting and significant opportunities, probably grateful that I was yet to mention the loud workmen.

'Don't you have an exam tomorrow?' she then asked.

Gah, it was true. Silly legal studies.

The next morning the men from the kitchen were gone, and my notes and books were back scattered across the table. My exam started in a few hours, but I was beaming with joy. *The Gap Year* was open in front of me, with different organisations highlighted in fluoro green. But none of them mattered anymore; I had just found the organisation for me—I was sure of it!

Student Partnerships Worldwide (SPW) offered volunteer opportunities in remote communities around the world. You worked with in-country volunteers for either five months on an agriculture-based project or eight months on a health-based project. It was perfect. It was actually perfect.

The health project appealed to me the most, simply because it was the longest of the two options. I raced to my room, grabbed my mobile phone, and returned to the book. The organisation's number was right there, waiting for me. I didn't hesitate in dialling. A woman with an English accent answered. I introduced myself and said that I wanted to volunteer for the health program, either in Tanzania or Kenya. I was talking quickly but I was unbelievably excited and in my mind I was already packing my bags. Once I finished my little monologue, the woman paused briefly and then apologised; applications had closed two months earlier.

My heart sunk. Of course there were other organisations, but applying for them now would be like having to eat Weetbix when I knew how good muesli tasted.

Suddenly I realised the time. I grabbed my books, jumped in my car and headed to my exam. We were herded into the exam room like cattle but when I sat down, my mind was in Africa. Nevertheless, I felt the exam went okay.

Afterwards there was the usual post-exam, comparing-answers chatter. I suddenly realised that I had misread one of the questions. If I had read it correctly I could have given the perfect answer, but instead I had written something completely off topic. I should have been more stressed than I was, but I actually felt more disappointed for my legal studies teacher.

'You know Mrs Edwards thinks you're home studying hard,' my English teacher had said to me the week before when he saw me at work in the bakery.

I had used SWOTVAC as an opportunity to pick up more shifts and save funds for when I eventually worked out what I was going to do in my gap year. I had told my English teacher that my books were out the back. Not that they were much good to me there anyway. Mrs Edwards was also our careers counsellor and I found her advice heavily influenced by the fact that she was also my legal studies teacher. Naturally, she thought I should be a lawyer.

Everyone around me was in a huddle talking about the exam but I didn't want to get swept up into their state of anxiety. It was over. This was the time to rejoice, not wallow in regret. I said goodbye to my friends and went home.

I walked straight inside, went to the kitchen bench, grabbed *The Gap Year* and dialled the SPW number again. This time I went outside to talk—perhaps it was silly but I felt there was more positive energy outside. The same woman answered the phone and I quickly re-introduced myself—but this time I added that I had been working part-time for three years and had saved $10 000. I was really interested in human rights and was involved in an Amnesty International group at my school, I told her. I was very passionate about Africa. I understood that applications had closed, but I was asking them to make an exception.

The woman asked me to hold. I paced back and forth by the pool, waiting for the verdict. Then she came back on the line. 'There is training in Sydney in two weeks' time. Can you make it?'

'Yes!' I answered immediately. Go to the training, impress them, show how passionate you are.

Go to Africa—that was the plan.

●

When I went to Sydney for the SPW training, my friends were off at 'schoolies', celebrating the end of school. I felt like I should have cared that I was missing this week of youthful fun, but honestly I was relieved. I didn't like drinking that much, and my boyfriend had finished school the year before so it wasn't really his scene either. The training was actually convenient timing.

There were only a few of us there and only two of us wanted to go on the health program. Lindy, the other girl (really she was a woman, who I would later learn was 27) had a very peaceful and wise presence about her. She had my immediate respect and admiration. All the SPW staff were lovely, and the training felt more like relaxed conversations.

They decided that I could go to Africa, but there was only room for me on the placement in Uganda. I had barely heard of Uganda, but I happily agreed anyway.

That afternoon, I celebrated by getting my first vaccinations. I had two in one arm, and one in the other. I would have to have many more before I left Australia. I would also need to organise malaria tablets and come up with some extra cash. The placement cost $12 000, $5000 of which was a compulsory donation.

Back home in Adelaide, Mum and Dad were extremely supportive. Mum even managed to laugh. She said it was in my nature to pick the most challenging thing possible, in a place we had hardly heard of. Of course I could also see the worry in her eyes, but at the time neither of us mentioned it. I had inherited my adventurous spirit and my stubbornness from Dad, so I think he knew there was no point trying to change my mind. Better to support me than to argue—either way, I was going to go.

For Mum, I knew it was harder. I imagined her restless at night, feeling anxious about her daughter taking off. Later she would tell me that others had criticised her as a mother—my nanna had told her to put her foot down. I knew that my mum must have loved me so much to still want me to go. She could see me glowing with joy and she would do everything in her power to help me, regardless of how scared she felt or what anyone said.

My boyfriend, Jack, was also unbelievably supportive and I realised that he too must have cared for me deeply, to put my happiness before his own. We planned to have a long distance relationship while I was away; we never even discussed anything else. Secretly, I worried that being apart for so long would be too hard, but then I remembered the wind. I told myself that I did not need to see Jack to feel his love. I hoped desperately that this was true. I never even considered that it might be my feelings that would change.

As I began to get things organised for my trip, I felt like I was in a constant state of motion. I raised the extra money I needed by getting donations from Rotary and Lions clubs (I would have to do presentations for them on my return), by asking family friends for donations and by selling cakes during our School Awards Night. Mum stood behind the trestle table with me in the foyer, collecting people's money and counting out their change.

The bakery I worked at had donated the cakes. Jack's dad was a milkman and he also asked his customers for donations, which was a lovely gesture. It felt like all the important people in my life were coming together to help me pursue this dream.

I had my extra injections, and began my malaria tablets as I was required to start taking them before I actually got there. I bought a mosquito net (which I would later realise was stupid as they were sold *everywhere* in Uganda), a new red backpack, a pair of brown leather sandals from the camping store and a head torch (which would prove to be my most useful possession). I also packed eight months' worth of tampons. We had been advised about this at the training—such things were hard, if not impossible, to come by in Uganda.

I was all set, but the funny thing was that I was so consumed with the thought of getting to Africa that I had given very little thought to the life I was leaving behind me. Mum would have to pack my things in boxes after the house was sold, and put them into storage. I would not be coming back to my family home; maybe I would not even come home to my family. At that time they might still be living in Ireland. But admittedly it was not really this that was upsetting me—it was the reality of leaving Jack.

The morning I was set to fly out, I woke up before my alarm. I had hardly slept I was so restless. I had half been wishing time away, but then suddenly never wanting the night to end—I didn't want to say goodbye. And now it was actually time to get up. To get organised. To go. Jack was peacefully asleep beside me and, without intending to, I started crying. *What am I doing? I have a good life. I could stay in Australia, start university, travel with Jack.* No, my heart said, that's not who you are and that's not what you really want. It was strange for my heart to feel so strongly about going, even though my mind and body now wanted me to stay.

I decided it was easiest to get up and start getting ready before Jack woke. I snuck into the shower and when I returned to my room, dressed in my pre-planned airport outfit, he was sitting up in bed. I nearly cried again, but stopped myself. Instead, I made a comment about how ridiculous I felt. I was wearing way too many layers of clothing, plus my hiking boots, because everything wouldn't fit into my bag. It wasn't exactly a comfortable travelling outfit.

Jack managed a smile, then he too got up and got ready. It was amazing how, even when filled with the strongest of emotions, we were able to go about such normal morning rituals.

Mum, Dad and both my brothers were coming to the airport to see me off. Because we wouldn't all fit in the car, Jack and I drove separately. I found myself thinking about my room. I suddenly felt like I should have studied it more closely before I left, or taken a photograph or something. It was so 'my room'. It was painted just the way I had wanted (the bottom half blue and the top sandy yellow, as if I were living on the beach), with wooden beams running across the top and on them artificial rock-climbing holds. I used to be able to swing from hold to hold, and reach the window sill from my bed without my feet touching the ground.

The other special place in my room was the top of the built-in wardrobe. I couldn't reach there using my rock-climbing holds, so I would pull the wooden drawers from the wardrobe half out and climb them like a ladder. Then I would sit up there and make engravings on a separate wooden beam that ran parallel to the top of the wardrobe. I had been climbing up there since I was just a little kid. That wooden beam had engraved into it the name of the first boy I had had a crush on. And all my friends' names too—I used to make them climb up there as their initiation into my room. I also used to steal food from the kitchen and hide it there. Things that Mum wouldn't suspect, like the gelatine crystals for the jelly. The thought of my room and its many memories made me smile. And then it made me sad—it wasn't my room anymore and I would never see it again.

I had known this before, of course, but I hadn't really considered it until now. Jack noticed my silence and asked if I was excited. I think he was trying to cheer me up. I smiled, but I didn't answer. I wouldn't have known what to say—I was excited, but I was also terrified. The wild contrast in my emotions made me confused.

We got to the airport earlier than necessary, checked in my baggage and went through security. Josh was complaining that he was hungry and thirsty, so Dad suggested we have breakfast in one of the cafes. I don't remember what we ate; I just recall the uneasy silence. The feeling when you know something terrible is about to happen. And then it did happen—my flight number was called. The voice on the loudspeaker seemed to echo through me—it was time to board. I started crying even while I was still walking to the departure gate.

On the way, Jack suddenly started pulling me. I looked at him questioningly and he pointed to a little photo booth. It was one of those where you go in, it takes a shot and then prints the photo as a series of little stickers; in the backdrop is a shark about to swallow you whole, or something like that.

'We don't have time,' I said, a little pissed off.

But Jack insisted. He dragged me into the booth, pulled the booth curtain shut, and kissed me passionately. He hadn't wanted the photo stickers at all. All he wanted was a final moment with just us. I wanted to stay in that moment forever, but I really had to go.

We got to my gate and everyone was already boarding. I felt annoyed at myself that we had spent so much time in the silly cafe and now had to say goodbye so quickly. This was it. I said goodbye to my family first. Sam seemed quite indifferent to me leaving: 'Have a good trip, Nik.' Josh gave me more attention, giving me a big hug, but I wasn't sure he really understood what was going on. The hug with Dad was brief and slightly awkward—hugging wasn't something we did a lot. And then there was Mum. She had started crying while I was still hugging Josh. 'You know me'—she tried to make a joke of her emotional state. It was true that she was a highly emotional person; she could cry during cartoons. This time, however, her tears were justified. She hugged me tightly and it was difficult to let go. When I finally pulled away, she reached into her handbag and handed me a letter: 'Read it on the plane.' We both expressed ourselves better through written words. I put the letter safely in my bag.

Next was Jack. It was horrible. We were both crying as we hugged. I remember thinking that the other passengers must have thought we were being over-dramatic, given that this flight was just to Sydney. I wanted to tell them that I was actually going a whole world away, and that I was terrified. But instead I hugged my brothers, Dad, Mum and Jack once more. And then, like a lemming, I joined the boarding queue with everyone else.

As I was having my ticket checked, I took a final look back at the most important people in my life. Jack had put his sunglasses on to hide his wet eyes, but I could still imagine their radiant blue. Josh was hugging Mum now—he was probably telling her to stop crying. Sam and Dad stood with their hands in their pockets, not knowing what to do with themselves in such an emotionally charged situation. I started walking down towards the aerobridge ramp. The walkway was parallel to where my family and Jack were standing, with only a glass barrier separating us. I imagined them watching me, so close and yet untouchable. I could have faced them while I was walking, I could have pressed my hand against the glass, I could have stayed a moment longer. But then I don't know that I would have ever left, so I kept walking. I kept walking and I didn't look back.

On the plane I was forced to compose myself. I had a window seat and I stared out at Adelaide. As the plane took off, I watched everything that was familiar become no more than a Lego world. Looking at it like that, it seemed that I could build my city in a matter of minutes. I imagined myself picking up each building, every tree and such, and fitting them all into the palm of my hand. People were soon the size of grains of sand, and they filled in the gaps between the imaginary city now nestled in my palm. With the life I knew so well safely in my grasp now, I decided to put it into my pocket and carry it with me.

It was a good thing I did this, because soon we were among the clouds—Adelaide was gone. I told myself I could recreate it anytime. I could pull it out of my pocket, imagine it all unfolding. I told myself that I never really had to leave anywhere, because my thoughts could always carry me back. And then, feeling much calmer, I pulled Mum's letter out of my bag and started to read it.

3
The North Star

JINJA, UGANDA, January 2005

From Adelaide I flew to Sydney and then to Dubai, Nairobi and finally Entebbe, where Uganda's airport was based. Flying over Uganda was magical. It didn't look like a Lego world, even when everything was so distant and small. It was too green, too real; there were too many interesting shapes for it to be compared to childhood building blocks.

As our plane dropped lower in the late afternoon, Uganda's magic and beauty intensified, as did my smile. Walking off the plane was a surreal experience. I had been dreaming of Africa since I was just a kid, when I had thought it was a country rather than a continent. And suddenly here I was, my feet stepping on African soil for the first time. Unbelievable. The humidity hit my skin instantly and I loved it. I breathed in the fresh air, the smell of trees. I flung my head up to the welcoming blue sky, my smile stretched across my face. I had made it.

Walking toward the airport, a tin shed, I gazed through the windows and saw dozens of African children smiling and waving. I had no idea what they were doing there—maybe they were the children of the airport staff—but I could not have imagined a more perfect first impression of the country.

I was full of joy but also anxious. Who really knew if this SPW organisation actually existed? It was Mum's voice I was hearing in my mind now. As I picked up my luggage, I noticed three Ugandans, two males and a female, wearing oversized white T-shirts with blue print that read 'SPW'. Perfect. I introduced myself and followed the SPW staff outside, where they had a vehicle waiting. I couldn't help noticing that one of them, Charles, was abnormally tall, stick thin, with a long face. He reminded me of a giraffe. He also had a really big goofy smile. I decided immediately that he was most likely the friendliest of this trio.

We clambered into a 4WD and were on our way. The driving was mental, completely chaotic. At first I tried to work out whether there was any system to the chaos, but my attention quickly became focused elsewhere. I was shocked to see so much poverty, literally only a street away from the airport. It made me think of World Vision television adverts; I could have taken all that footage in the first 10 minutes.

I saw women carrying enormous loads on their heads, such as bags of potatoes. I saw young children with skinny arms and legs and pot bellies—signature signs of malnourishment—washing their clothes in a basin. I saw bulls, and goats and chickens roaming freely.

Occasionally there were large billboards on the side of the road. Most of them had advertisements but some were government funded. One read: 'Having sex with a virgin will not cure AIDS'. My heart stopped for a moment and my mouth went dry. Obviously many people seriously believed that having sex with a virgin *would* cure AIDS. Such ignorance seemed terrifying.

It was difficult to comprehend that the village where I would be living and working would be even more poverty-stricken. As we continued on our way, the shapes around me became mere silhouettes as darkness descended and scared the sun away. Everyone in the car was silent and I appreciated being left alone with my thoughts. We were heading to a boarding school about two hours away, where all the new volunteers would have three weeks' training before being split up and allotted to our different placements.

My companions informed me that all the other international volunteers and the Ugandan volunteers were already at the boarding school, and would probably be asleep when we arrived. By then I was too tired to care. Over 40 hours of travel was starting to take its toll.

When we finally arrived, I was directed through the darkness to the room where I would sleep. It was a shed with a tin roof but fortunately it had lots of windows. There were seven beds in the room, and all except for one were full of bodies peacefully asleep in the cocoons of their mosquito nets.

As I slid into the empty bed, doubt followed in after me. I didn't question my desire to be in this magical, mysterious place; I questioned what I had to contribute. For a time I could not get to sleep, which was odd. *How can I now be this awake,* I thought, *when only minutes ago I was dead tired? What if I don't ever get to sleep and am then exhausted for the first day of training? What if I fall asleep in the training? I'm never going to fall asleep.*

And then I woke up. Sunlight crept through the numerous windows, as did the sounds of various unknown animals making their morning calls. As I peered through my mozzie net and out the window opposite my bed, I saw pure green—what a lush, beautiful country I was in. Looking out the window behind my bed, I saw young Ugandan children playing and laughing; their smiles were big and uplifting. I felt good. The joyful sounds and images from outside were enough to extinguish, at least temporarily, my anxieties from the night before.

There was a toilet and shower—although I was not convinced they were worthy of such titles—attached to our room. The toilet was a hole in the ground but not your typical long drop, as it still seemed to have a flush. I used most of my strength to pull down the flushing lever—and was shocked when water sprayed absolutely everywhere!

I literally had to grab the toilet paper and run. I had a moment in which I was already starting to miss the luxuries of home, but things were certainly more entertaining this way. It was a bit of a game—how fast can you run? The shower also looked interesting but I wasn't game to try it on that first morning. Lindy, the only other Australian volunteer, had one and came out with giant ant bites on her feet—and she had been wearing shoes!

Our training started bright and early at 8:30 a.m. There was no time to adjust—it was as though I had woken up in a completely different life. I was suddenly in a brick building, with open spaces where there should have been doors and windows. Wooden tables and chairs formed a U shape facing the front of the room. I sat down and smiled at the volunteers sitting either side of me. The three staff who had picked me up the night before—Charles, Irene and Paul—were sitting up the front.

Paul stood up and, with a white stick of chalk in his hand, proceeded to write his name on the blackboard. Then he wrote 'Health Education'. We were to learn the basics for the material that we would be teaching in the local primary and secondary schools once we were sent to different villages for our placements. I glanced around the room. Strangers surrounded me. I had met some of the girls from my room earlier that morning but now, as I looked about, I struggled to remember anyone's name.

Paul began talking and I had to concentrate. I was not used to the Ugandan accent or their way of saying things. I had noticed immediately when I arrived in the country that a favourite Ugandan means of expression was to use 'and what?' mid-sentence. It was not intended as a question, but more as a conjunction, a joining word, like 'because'.

The staff started to go over basic information about AIDS and we did a session on facts and myths, such as *If a boy does not have sex then his penis will shrink*. The SPW staff asked us whether we agreed with this statement. One of the Ugandan volunteers said that he disagreed. Then, as his grin grew, he glanced down before exclaiming, 'Some things are just naturally big. If you are small, you are small; and if you are big, you are BIG!'

I couldn't help myself from smiling; Irene noticed this and gave me daggers. I bit my bottom lip and turned away from her to face one of the other Ugandan volunteers, who actually agreed with the myth and was unselfconsciously elaborating on his own experiences. He didn't seem to realise that the penis is always smaller when not erect; he thought his penis was permanently shrinking. Luke, the only male international volunteer, was sitting next to the Ugandan who was talking. Luke's teeth-displaying grin seemed to take up his whole face. When I saw it, I suddenly felt ashamed of my own little smile.

The Ugandan volunteers were being so honest and it was interesting how uncomfortable that made us international volunteers feel. Health education was a part of our school curriculum in Australia, but not part of the school curriculum in Uganda. Yet here I was blushing like a little schoolgirl at the mention of the word penis. I felt embarrassed for feeling embarrassed! How ridiculous. What made such honesty all the more amusing was that all the Ugandans pronounced penis as *pen-is* (as though to rhyme with Dennis). If one of the international volunteers spoke and pronounced the word differently, Paul would correct them. Which was another reason I wanted to keep my mouth shut.

I sat very quietly and began to observe the intriguing little critters that seemed to be appearing all around the room. The lizards, in particular, seemed to be having a blissful time crawling along the bricks before disappearing outside.

●

Our training was at a boarding school, so there were kids everywhere even though it was school holidays. The kids loved the international volunteers and found us hilarious. They could not understand a word we said—perhaps that's why they found us so funny. They would call out to us and wave, gesturing us over to play with them. They loved having their photo taken and were fascinated to see their image in the digital camera. I got the impression that many of them were seeing themselves for the first time. Pretty crazy.

I began to learn the children's names; recognising them was made easier because they wore the same clothes every day. It made me think about when I had been packing, about how I had spent so much time trying to work out which of my zillions of things were appropriate. In the end I had actually bought new tank tops and shorts to bring. Now I played with children who literally only had the clothes on their back. Poverty slapped me in the face wherever I looked.

The food was different to anything I was used to. It was all very heavy but most of it was vegetarian, which was a relief as I didn't eat meat. I tried bits of everything and liked a dish with beans the best. We ate all our meals together in a large room with big pots of different things up the front for us to help ourselves from. Breakfast was my favourite as we got fresh fruit—the pineapple was the sweetest I had ever tasted. Mealtime was also the most social time. There were many different characters in our group but, while I was enjoying everyone's company, I missed Jack a lot. When my mind went wandering, it often found its way back to him.

One morning, a group from The AIDS Support Organisation (TASO), the largest AIDS support organisation in Uganda, came to speak with us. There were five women in the group; all were HIV positive. Obviously I had heard about HIV and AIDS before, but I had not really understood it clearly until now. In a nutshell, HIV is the virus that attacks the immune system, and AIDS is the series of diseases and infections that occur as a result. I could have googled these facts on the internet, but it was different when someone who was living with HIV was sitting in front of you, telling you their story.

The women were just skin and bone, and their colourful clothes hung off them. They looked fragile and vulnerable. The women were all softly spoken and their words came out slowly, as if speaking was a struggle. They spoke in their village languages and Irene translated. One woman explained how her husband had died of AIDS. She said that they were from a poor village and he had been scared to be tested for

HIV because he would not know what to do if he tested positive. He became increasingly ill, and she ended up persuading him to be tested. His worst fears were confirmed. The local medical clinic was supposed to provide him with antiretroviral treatment but the clinic was under-resourced and he never received the treatment he needed. His wife, as well as looking after their four children, had cared for him selflessly until he passed away. She was then tested herself. When her results were positive, she knew she could not rely on the local clinic so she had left the village with her children and found TASO and had been receiving treatment and support since. Her body shook slightly as she spoke. Her skin was shrivelled and she looked quite old, but perhaps her body was just weathered from hardship.

Once the woman had finished her story she asked us to stand up and form a circle. We clambered over the tables, and formed a circle in the middle of the room. The five women from TASO joined us, and we all held hands. One of the women was holding one of my hands. I was surprised by how firm her grasp was. I knew it was not possible, but it was as if I could feel her heartbeat through her hand. And her heart felt strong.

The women started singing. Their voices were much louder now than when they had spoken. Through their words earlier, I had felt each woman's anguish in trying to survive on her own. But when they sang together, they formed one voice and it was unbelievably powerful.

●

On another day we were learning about teaching techniques, and again I was spending more time watching the various bugs crawl and in and out of the room. I wanted to pay attention but Paul would tell us what he was going to tell us, and then he would tell us, and then he would tell us what he had told us. And he seemed to go through that whole process about three times every time, just to make a simple point.

I was getting agitated and bored but then Luke raced into the room, looking dishevelled and anxious. He announced that he was late because he had been looking for his phone but hadn't been able to find it. And then he had realised that he also couldn't find his wallet. He had finally concluded that both had been stolen. Irene instructed Luke to take a *matatu* into Jinja, the nearest big town, and go to the police station. I was surprised that none of the staff offered to go with him, but he didn't seem bothered and went on his way. Paul then went back to explaining the same point that he had been making for the last half an hour, and I sat wishing I were outside playing with the kids in the beautiful sunshine.

When the training finally ended for the day, we all retreated to our rooms. I sat on my bed, exhausted from doing absolutely nothing. Suddenly I realised that my money belt, which had previously been in my bag, was lying on the floor. I grabbed it—the zip was open and all my money was gone. I had probably lost about $500. A sigh of disappointment then came from the other side of the room as Jane realised that her camera was missing. All the other girls started searching through their stuff, but they all seemed to be okay.

Jane and I caught a *matatu* into Jinja and then walked to the police station. By the time we got there, it was about 7 p.m. They were not impressed that we had turned up at such an hour, but they agreed, rather hesitantly, to speak to us anyway.

Luke must have already completed his statement as we didn't see him at the station. Jane and I followed a plump little policeman to the interview room. Walking down the narrow corridor we passed one of the prison cells. There were only boys in the cell; they had little clothing, and they were shouting and reaching out to us through the metal bars.

I hadn't anticipated there would be a prison cell inside the police station and it caught me off guard. The boys would have been my own age or younger but when they called out to me, their hands twisting through the bars and reaching out towards me, I felt anxious and I hurried past them. But any anxiety I had quickly turned into amusement as Jane and I took our seats in the cement block of an interview room. The policeman plonked himself down behind his wooden desk on which bits of paper were scattered about. The walls were bare except for a large piece of brown paper. On it was written a guide for how to proceed with an interview. It looked as if a child just starting to learn to write had written it:

A Guide for Interviewing
Just remember the 5 W's
WHO?
WHERE?
WHAT?
WHEN?
WHY?

The policeman, who was dressed in simple black pants and a shirt, began to ask us the 5 Ws and I tried to focus and answer him sensibly. He seemed to have a twitch and his head kept jerking to the left. He was also intently scratching his right ear. I felt disconcerted and distracted. Then everything went black.

Blackouts were a common occurrence in Jinja and probably in every other town in Uganda too. The policeman informed us that we would have to come back in the morning. Almost as soon as we left, the power flicked back on. However, the policeman had firmly shut the station's door, so Jane and I decided to make the most of being in town, and found a small shop where we could use the internet. I couldn't help noticing heads turn as Jane and I entered and asked if there were any spare computers. Jinja was the hub for white-water rafting expeditions or for tourists passing through on an East African tour but not many foreigners actually ate local food or went into local shops, such as this one. Jane and I stood out like snow in a desert and people seemed both curious and sceptical at our presence.

I took a seat in front of a computer and tried to ignore the man sitting next to me, who was not at all embarrassed to be staring directly at me. Instead, I focused on my computer but the internet connection was painfully slow. My heart was beating fast as I waited for my email account to open. I was desperate for news from Jack; I wanted to know anything and everything. *Hurry up! Hurry up, you silly thing!* I mentally abused the computer—imagining Jack's emails appearing in my inbox, I was beginning to get excited. Finally, my account started to open. Everything was downloading... and then: 'No new mail.' Nothing. I felt like bursting into tears. It had been a weird day and I just needed to feel some connection. It wasn't there. I emailed mum, logged out, and waited for Jane.

The next morning Jane, Luke and I made our way back to the police station with the aim of following up on our statements. The policeman from the previous night told us bluntly that we needed to wait. He didn't elaborate on what exactly we were waiting for. We waited for three hours, but nothing happened.

I was grateful to have Luke and Jane for company. Jane was English and Luke Canadian, and both of their accents amused me. Both also had wild curly hair, which I was quite jealous of. Other than that, the two couldn't have been more different. Luke seemed rough and arrogant and out of place. Jane seemed gentle, kind and intelligent. The three of us were chatting away when the policeman finally appeared and said he wanted to come to the boarding school to check things out. This seemed reasonable so we followed him outside. He announced that he didn't have a vehicle and called a taxi. He then sat in the front, while Jane, Luke and I piled in the back.

We were cruising along, the policeman chatting to the taxi driver in the local language, when suddenly the taxi stopped. I was squashed in the middle, so I peered around Luke to look out the window. I had no idea where we were. The policeman spun his head around to face us and as my eyes retreated from the window they were met by the policeman's intense stare. The night before, he had seemed almost vulnerable, with his head twitch and his ear scratching, but now his eyes looked different, darker. He demanded money. It was for the taxi fare, he declared. But then he added that if we did not hand over the cash for the taxi fare he would leave us here in the middle of nowhere. Blackmail. We reluctantly handed over some money, and fortunately the taxi driver proceeded to drive us to the boarding school. I began to wonder whether I would end up losing more money to the corrupt police than had actually been stolen.

During the policeman's investigations, I retreated to my room. I collapsed onto my bed, put my earphones in and let Missy Higgins calm my soul. A short time later Luke appeared at the door to our girls' room. 'Guess what the police found!' he exclaimed.

I pulled my earphones out and sat up. Luke came and sat on my bed, and then went into a ramble. He said the policeman had not discovered anything useful to help solve our theft, but he had found 12 passports hidden in the home of one of the women who lived at the boarding school. He had taken her back with him for questioning. Pretty bizarre—but nevertheless I hoped her journey would not be interrupted by some sly blackmail along the way.

Luke then asked what I was listening to. I gave him one of my earphones, while I put the other in my own ear. I handed Luke my iPod and let him flick through my various tunes. When we were alone together, I found him to be gentle, open and fun. But I had definitely sensed arrogance earlier, and wondered how he could be such a contrast of traits. I was pleasantly surprised to discover that Luke could not be as easily defined as I had initially thought. We sat together until dinnertime, when we went and joined the others for beans, rice, *matooke* (squashed green bananas) and ground nut sauce. I sat next to Jane and Lindy, and we laughed about the day's events. As we were talking, a bug crawled out of Lindy's beans. This caused further outbursts of giggles, but we all still went back for seconds.

The next morning we were informed that there was a suspect. On the day of the theft, a woman, claiming to be looking for a nurse, had entered the hallway to which the girls' room and the nurse's house were attached. The children had told the woman that the nurse was not in. The woman then clenched at her stomach and said she felt extremely ill. She asked the children for the key to the girls' room so she could lie down. The children, wanting to help, had fetched her the key. When the nurse arrived home, the woman had gone. And so too was my money and Jane's camera. We still didn't know how the woman also gained access to the boys' room to take Luke's things. The children recognised the woman as an SPW volunteer from the previous year, but the police were hopeless.

In the end it was Paul who played detective and solved the great mystery. He showed the children photos of all of the volunteers from the previous year and the children identified one of the Ugandan women as being the secret visitor the week earlier. Paul still had her address so he rocked up to her place; even from her doorway, he could see Jane's camera. Her theft plan had started brilliantly but she was quickly uncovered.

Jane got her camera back, and Luke his phone, but she had already spent my money and the money from Luke's wallet. To have executed such a plan, she was obviously desperate for cash so, even though I condemned stealing, I wasn't going to demand she give up the few things she owned in an attempt to pay me back. To me, a few hundred dollars was a safari; to her, it was probably paying for a younger sibling's school fees.

Luke's reaction was different. He was extremely pissed off and wanted to press charges. I have always thought that you can tell the most about someone not by how they treat those they love but by how they treat a complete stranger. His reaction was quite unsettling—he showed no empathy at all. He seemed set in his mind about what was right and wrong, and there was no room for shades of grey. I tried to tell myself that we each decide our own values and that Luke was entitled to feel the way he did. But, no matter how much I tried to understand his view, I still thought he was being unreasonable. I found his behaviour difficult to accept.

•

I was also struggling with the training. I found myself challenging everything, and this was causing problems with the SPW staff. Irene, especially, didn't like me. When she was teaching us, she would express her own opinion as though it was a fact; she talked as if there was only one way to teach and as if she wanted us to go out to our various placements as Irene clones. But I didn't want to be a robot. I actually wanted to use my brain and exercise some creativity. Irene wasn't interested in new ideas, however. She took a defensive position, which naturally made me the enemy. But sometimes when I questioned her, I was shocked by my own tone of voice. *Was I now the one being arrogant? Was Luke's behaviour bothering me so much because I saw traits of him in myself and I didn't like it?*

One afternoon I was relieved when the training was over for the day and decided to take my mind off things by washing my clothes. Grabbing my dirty things, I filled a basin under the shower and stood there scrubbing. This was the first time I'd washed all my clothes by hand. It proved a much-needed release of built-up frustration and was extremely satisfying. I had nearly finished this task when something hit my back. I felt water seeping through my shirt and cooling my skin. As I turned around, I came face to face with Natalie (a volunteer from the UK) and a grinning Luke. Both of them were armed with more water bombs which they hurled towards me.

Before I could respond, they both suddenly tackled me where I was and then turned the shower on full force. Now I was in hysterics. Were they tackling me or tickling me? It didn't matter. I didn't care. I was drenched, and all my other clothes were also wet from having just been washed. I walked to dinner soaked, water dripping off my hair and down my face. When I entered the room, Irene looked at me in disgust but I couldn't hide my smile—I was deliriously happy.

Every night, once each of us girls had tucked our mozzie nets under our mattresses and the main lights had been turned out, we would enter our own little world. Some would flick torches on and scribble in their diaries or read novels; others seemed to drift peacefully to sleep as soon as their heads hit their pillows.

On this particular evening I had my earphones in again, with Missy Higgins singing softly. Her album was on shuffle and my eyelids were growing heavy when the track '10 Days' began.

As I listened, I realised that I had been away from home exactly ten days. As the song continued, tears dropped from my heavy eyes.

I wasn't crying because I missed home. I was crying because I didn't miss it, or not as much as I felt I should anyway. I had only been here ten days and yet already this place—which was still so intriguing and so full of uncertainty—felt more like home than Australia. I think it was the unpredictability that I was drawn to. I went to sleep every night with no idea what the next day would hold, and I *loved* that.

I brushed my tears away with my arm, quietly pulled my mozzie net out from the mattress, and snuck outside. I felt guilty about how much I was enjoying the changes that were happening in my life. For the last few nights I had taken to sitting outside and staring at the Southern Cross. When there were no phone calls, no emails, I would look at this constellation and tell myself that this was something that connected me to Australia, to Jack.

As I crept outside on this night and gazed up to the stars, one star was shining brighter than all the others. It was magnificent. And then I realised—I was looking at the North Star. On every previous night I had been so distracted by the Southern Cross that I had completely forgotten that Uganda was on the equator. Now I stood bewildered. My eyes drifted between the North Star and the Southern Cross: my new life and my old one. Finally my eyes rested on the North Star. Perhaps because it was new and different and exciting. Or maybe just because it really was the brightest star I had ever seen.

4

A Magical Place

JINJA—NAMWENDWA, UGANDA, February 2005

After stuffing my face with *matooke* and groundnut sauce, I was walking back to the training room for the afternoon session when I passed Luke talking on his phone. His voice sounded frustrated. I knew that I should have just kept walking, but my feet were operating against my will and had slowed to a snail-like pace. I realised that Luke was on the phone to his dad, and it sounded like they were arguing about the theft and the pressing of charges. It dawned on me that perhaps it wasn't Luke's arrogance that I had heard earlier. Maybe he didn't want to press charges at all, but his dad was pressuring him to do so. Then again, perhaps I was just interpreting things the way I wanted to. Admittedly, my feelings about Luke were becoming increasingly biased.

We didn't have training on the weekends and so this was our time to explore our surroundings. Luke was desperate to get his phone unlocked so he could buy a Ugandan SIM card but nowhere in Jinja was he able to do so. He had decided that he was going to take the bus to Kampala, the capital of Uganda, to find a place able to help him. He invited me to come along for the ride. I was not a fan of big towns, but I was curious to see how Kampala compared to Jinja.

It was only a few hours on the bus and, as I'd suspected, I didn't like Kampala. It was a big, dirty city. But we found somewhere that said they could help Luke with his phone, so we felt we had achieved our mission. The sales assistant said it would take an hour, so we wandered the streets and had lunch. As we were walking back, we discovered an ice-cream shop. We hadn't had any treats since we had arrived in Uganda, so we indulged. We still had our ice-creams in our hands when we got back to the phone place, but the woman who had first talked to us now apologised and said they had a small problem. They had successfully unlocked Luke's phone, but in the process all the numbers that had been saved to it had been lost.

This news didn't go down well and Luke started yelling at the woman. I felt awful for her. Surely Luke could just email home and get the numbers again? I was starting to feel seriously uncomfortable and to think that my first impression of Luke had actually been spot-on. But as I went to turn away from him, he caught me by surprise and dabbed the tip of his ice-cream onto my nose. And then there was that smile. We both burst out laughing. Suddenly Luke seemed to forget the problem with his phone and we left the shop.

On the bus back, we were both listening to his iPod, with an earplug each. I was becoming tired and, without thinking, rested my head on his shoulder. It felt like the natural thing to do. I had my eyes closed, but I nonetheless felt it when he placed his hand on my knee. I liked it.

The next day I entered the training room and sat down. Irene, Paul and Charles were already sitting at the front, and Irene had a very sly grin on her face. I had a feeling that something terrible was about to happen. The other volunteers sat down, and everyone seemed to notice the unexplained tension in the air. We sat silently, staring at the SPW staff expectantly.

It was Paul who stood first to speak. He seemed to like being the one in control. He announced that they had decided who each of us would be on placement with. My heart started pounding uncontrollably. Charles then stood up as well. He and Paul spent many minutes joking around with each other, teasing us. They were toying with our feelings, it seemed, amused by how easily we had become putty in their hands. I felt overwhelmed with nerves. Tears were forming behind my eyes. Unintentionally, I found myself sneaking glances at Luke. He still had that big goofy grin on his face and I almost felt pissed off that he didn't appear anxious at all.

Finally, Charles handed Paul the piece of paper that said it all. Paul glanced at the paper, and then at us, enjoying a final moment of power. Then he started to read. There would be two international volunteers and two Ugandan volunteers on each placement. He read out the first village placement name and then, painfully slowly, announced which volunteers would be living and teaching there.

I started crying. *How embarrassing*. I am such a product of my parents—I was pissed off, as I imagined Dad would be in this situation, and also an emotional wreck, just like Mum. The truly ridiculous part was that Paul hadn't even said my name. I was just so stressed that my emotions were swamping my sense of reason. That seemed to happen a lot to me in those days. I thought of myself as being a relaxed person, and yet here I was with my head buried in my hands, tears flowing, while surrounded by people in exactly the same situation, who were completely calm.

Paul paused again and looked up at me. I imagined that my thoughts were written all over my face. I had a tendency to be totally transparent, regardless of whether I wanted to be or not. Finally, he remembered that he was mid-sentence and continued talking. 'Namwendwa—Nikki, Jane, Lillian and Wemusa.'

I repeated his words in my head. My first thought was *not Luke, I wasn't with Luke*. My second thought was *Stop crying! Act happy! ACT HAPPY!* Deep breaths. *Think rationally.* Better.

I was actually pleased to be with Jane. I respected and trusted her. She was also a little bit older, 22, and I was grateful knowing I would always have her support. Lillian was very open and friendly, and while I didn't know her well,

I imagined that we would get along. Wemusa, however, I was very disappointed to be placed with. I had previously told the SPW staff that I definitely did not want to be placed with him. He was a very serious young man. He wore a suit every day to our training and believed firmly in formal teaching practices. I, on the other hand, wore flowing skirts and thought creativity was the most effective way to empower students to learn. I suspected that our differences would go far beyond our dress codes and teaching ideals.

After Paul had finished reading out our names, Irene almost jumped out of her seat. It was obvious she had been waiting for this moment. 'Nikki is clearly upset,' she said, trying to conceal a smile, 'but we couldn't make everyone happy.'

Thanks, Captain Obvious. Then she gave me a mango. A mango! I loved mangos but, please, it was more than a little patronising and it all got stuck in my teeth, making me an even bigger mess.

Tired of my emotions being used for the entertainment of SPW staff, I caught a *matatu* into town and went straight to a shop with the internet. This time hope didn't even rise in me as I waited for my email account to open. When my inbox downloaded and I had eight new emails, I was surprised more than delighted. Jack's email account had been down the previous week, and he had now compensated with numerous messages. He said all the conventionally right things—how much he missed me and was thinking of me—and I really wished I felt the same way. But I didn't.

Part of me wondered whether I had always known that I didn't feel a truly strong connection with Jack and that

I had tried to convince myself otherwise. Originally, I had desperately wanted a boyfriend—it felt like all the other girls had one. And then Jack had appeared. He was a year older and had a car, which had instantly made him cool. And he was cute and romantic. But, most significantly, he liked *me*. Goofy, stubborn, nerdy me.

It was difficult to answer this honestly, but was it Jack that I had actually liked, or just that feeling of being wanted? I didn't really know what I felt anymore. Sometimes it seemed like I missed Jack but I only felt that way when I was lonely. When I was happy or busy, he didn't cross my mind. It wasn't him I missed; it was knowing that someone was there for me.

The only thing that Jack and I ever had in common was each other. People say that opposites attract, and maybe for us that was true initially. But when there are no passions or activities to share, what is the glue that holds a relationship together? I didn't know. But I did know there was never anything wrong with our relationship, except for the very fact that it wasn't right.

Shit. I really wasn't ready for life-changing insights right now. I told myself that it wasn't fair to Jack to end our relationship via email. But that was bullshit. The truth was I was too scared, too selfish, to let him go and have to face the big scary world on my own. I denied my emotions, ignored Jack's emails and emailed my parents instead. I anticipated that this would be the last contact that I would have with them for a month or so. I would leave for my placement tomorrow. At least I now had the name of the village where I would be working and imagined Mum would find reassurance in being able to pinpoint me on a map.

•

That night, just after I had tucked my mozzie net in, Luke appeared. The main lights were still on but it was bedtime, not an appropriate hour for visiting. My eyes flickered around at the other girls but they were so absorbed in their own nightly rituals that they had barely glanced up when Luke entered. The SPW staff would definitely not approve of him lingering about our room but they already hated me and it was our last night of training. I lifted my mozzie net to say hello, and invited Luke into my little world. He climbed under the net and pulled the sheet over himself. We lay opposite each other, so close that our noses were touching.

Since two weeks earlier when Luke had first sat on my bed and listened to my iPod, we had taken to sharing our time and our music. He had become the companion that I needed, but tonight everything was different. Words were unnecessary because we both knew that tomorrow we would be separated by our different placements, and we would no longer be able to share anything.

Luke curled my hair around his fingers playfully. Then he gently stroked my face. Suddenly the main lights went out. The room was seductively dark but some of the girls still had torches on, so there was just enough light for me to see Luke's face. I wondered whether the girls realised that he was still in our room, in *my* bed, but I was enjoying myself too much to care. Under the sheet, my feet rubbed against Luke's. His toes were still cold from being outside. This was a new dynamic to our friendship . . . but I liked it. I had been craving this intimacy.

My hands were curled up in front of my face. Luke took them in his own hands, running his fingers through mine. His face dropped so it was resting on our hands, our eyes were locked as he lightly kissed each of my fingers. His lips were soft. My eyes were looking into his. Surely he was going to kiss me . . .

A little battle was going on inside my head. One moment I was urgently wanting him to kiss me; the next I was not so sure. Jack was still my boyfriend, regardless of how my feelings might have changed. But, I told myself my feelings *had* changed, and it was hard to be restrained just because that was supposedly the right thing to do. Then I remembered that there were six other girls in this room, all trying to sleep. Both my morals and my logic were screaming at me to do the same—and they overpowered my desire. But I still didn't have the willpower to ask Luke to leave.

I let my eyes drift away from him, which was enough for him to know that not all of me was in this moment. I wished him goodnight and fell asleep. By morning he was gone.

When the time came to say goodbye I wrapped my arms around Luke. Our whole group was breaking up and we all had to go our separate ways. I didn't want to let go of him.

Everyone was saying their farewells and so no-one seemed to notice that I hugged him for perhaps a few moments longer than I should have. Then I pulled myself away and joined Jane and Lillian on the back of a ute. Wemusa had already climbed into the front seat. Someone from the village was supposed to have picked us up, but they'd never arrived and so Paul had decided to just drive us there himself.

I felt unsure about the whole situation. Surely, if the community wanted us there, they would have come and collected us. It felt intrusive to be planning to rumble into a remote village in a loud ute. But admittedly I was enjoying the ride. I liked being bumped about, and having my hair thrashed about my face. Being outside always made me feel so alive.

The closer we drew to the village, the more beautiful our surroundings became. It was unbelievably green. I was sitting, resting against my backpack, and as I tilted my head, the sky was a perfect blue. We hadn't even arrived and already I felt an attachment to this place that was impossible to describe. It was enchanting, magical in the simplicity of its beauty. Mud huts with thatched roofs were scattered along the side of the road. I stood up to try to see how far back the huts went, but fields of crops blocked my view. Suddenly the ute sunk into a pothole and then hauled out of it. I nearly fell over, so I decided to sit down again.

I could hear children's voices shouting. I looked behind us—little legs chased after the ute as their equally little arms reached out to us in excitement. I waved to the children, my smile taking over my face. I looked at Jane, whose smile was as wide as my own, her eyes glistening with joy and warmth.

Lillian, too, was laughing. Her family home was not far from Namwendwa, and the surroundings were familiar to her, but sharing them was a new and exciting experience for her.

The ute stopped. Paul and Wemusa got out, and we followed suit by climbing off the back. A Ugandan man wandered up to us. He wore a smile and yet he threw his hands up to his face in despair as he approached. 'Welcome, welcome,' he said, moving his hands from his face.

He introduced himself as Andrew Opio, a teacher at Namwendwa primary school. He went on to explain that he had thought he was supposed to pick us up the following week. I was relieved to know that at least the community was expecting us. Wemusa, Lillian, Jane and I introduced ourselves; Andrew shook each of our hands with great enthusiasm.

Many people had now gathered around and were watching us with curiosity as we stood at the side of the ute. Andrew pointed in front of us and announced that this was our home. It was the end section of a cement block that seemed to be divided by cement walls. At the opposite end of this block was a small shop that Andrew said he owned. In front of our home was dirt and then a small grass patch and a little tree. A dusty road ran in front of our house and on the other side of that was a brick home with spaces where there should have been a door and window frames. To the left of our house were some small bushes and trees. Mud huts were scattered around.

I couldn't tell much else about our house from that distance except that it was small. Extremely small. Because its two wooden doors were padlocked shut, blocking us from entering, Andrew asked some children to go and find the landlord for the key. As soon as they scampered off, Paul, deciding that his job was now done, climbed back into the ute and disappeared.

A small boy soon returned holding the house key and Andrew performed the grand opening. He swung the doors open and my jaw dropped ever so slightly. Our house was chock-a-block full of maize and bags of charcoal. Andrew looked embarrassed. He must have forgotten that it was being used for storage.

As we all stood outside, looking at each other and wondering what to do next, it started to rain. Uganda is a tropical country and the rain proved a testament to that—it pounded down, loud and fast. We were all drenched, and my spirits too were starting to dampen. But then men and boys from the village suddenly appeared all around us. They began to work together, carrying all the maize and charcoal outside, as Andrew directed them. We were strangers in this place, and yet already everyone was so willing to help us.

Within ten minutes, the house was cleared and Andrew gestured us inside. The wooden doors opened to the main room, which had two smaller rooms attached, each with a wooden door. Imagine a cement block divided into a rectangle and two squares—that was our home. It had a cement floor and a tin roof, unlike the majority of houses in the village that generally had dirt floors and thatched roofs. As soon as we entered, children followed in after us carrying wooden chairs. They placed them down, and then disappeared back outside. Andrew also left, hurrying out into the rain, laughing, and saying that he needed to organise some things.

We sat down in the main room and tried to talk but the sound of the rain smashing against the tin roof was deafening. We were forced to sit in silence as we watched the dirt outside turn to mud. But I liked watching the rain; it was as enticing as the dancing flames of a fire.

When the sky finished its tantrum, Wemusa stood up and walked to the doorway of the room at the front of the house. He announced that this would be his room—a statement, not a question. The room he had chosen was the nicer of the two smaller rooms—it had the bigger window. The other room was not only smaller but the window was only slightly larger than an A4 piece of paper, which meant that even during the day the room was dark. Wemusa expected Jane, Lillian and me to share—squash into—this room. It seemed stupid and unfair, simply because he was male. But neither Jane nor Lillian mentioned it, so I didn't want to make a fuss either.

Later in the day, some boys brought us mattresses, leaning them against a wall in the main room. Jane and I tried to ask them where the mattresses were from but the boys looked at each other, confused. I wasn't sure if English was the problem or our accents. The boys stood there awkwardly, both desperate to get away, and when we thanked them, they shook their heads. 'Andrew,' they said, and then ran off outside.

Jane, Lillian and I tried to place our mattresses in our room but they wouldn't all fit—they overlapped each other and pushed up against the walls.

Just as it was getting dark, Andrew appeared carrying a kerosene lamp. He placed it on one of the wooden chairs in the main room. Once he had put the lamp down, I noticed that he was holding a plastic bag, from which he pulled out smaller bags, which he handed to each of us. My bag was warm and sweating. I opened it to discover beans and a *chapatti* (a savoury pancake). Andrew had bought us dinner! As we were still marvelling at the goods in our hands, Andrew called out to some children outside, asking them to bring more chairs, which they did. He sat and ate with us. We used our hands, tearing off pieces of the *chapatti* and using them to scoop up the beans.

When we finished, my hands were dirty. I tried to look at everyone else's, to see if they had created as much of a mess, but the light from the lamp was too faint to be able to tell. But then Andrew answered the question for me. He stood and disappeared outside; when he returned, he was carrying a jerry can. Calling us outside, he tilted the can and poured water over our hands for us to clean them. Then he asked Wemusa to hold the can while he washed his own hands. After this, he carried the jerry can inside and told us that it was ours to keep. He said that he would return in the morning and show us to the borehole. He would bring us a charcoal stove and organise bed frames for us. Then he wished us a good night.

Andrew had left us the lamp. We blew it out, and climbed into our beds. Despite my earlier concerns, it was actually quite fun being squashed in the room with the other girls, although we were a bit lopsided with the mattresses over-lapping each other. Jane and I were both wrapped in our sleeping bags and Lillian had a woollen blanket. As soon as we were all tucked in, Jane giggled. 'So, Luke?'

The three of us laughed. The girls had noticed Luke in my bed after all.

It was exciting to wake up and be able to race outside, our first real chance to see Namwendwa. About 10 metres behind our house was the community bathing area. It was just a small area with low walls made from bricks and an open doorway. People took it in turns to wash themselves, carrying in a full basin of water, which they carefully placed on the ground. They would strip off completely naked, splashing the water onto their bodies and scrubbing intensely. The area offered little privacy and I wondered whether the village people would be amused if they realised that in Australia we have not only at least one bathroom in each house but a lock on its door!

About 20 metres along from the bathing area was the community latrine. Fortunately, it had a roof and a door. The door didn't actually shut but this was perhaps for the best, given that the latrine absolutely stunk. It was used by about 30 people, including children who had a tendency to miss the hole. Unfortunately a lot of the children were sick with diarrhoea, which ended up in the spot where you needed to put your feet to squat.

I later discovered that it was best to go to the latrine early in the morning or in the late afternoon, because during the day there were so many flies swarming everywhere that you had to keep your mouth shut to stop them from buzzing inside. In the evenings the flies were gone, but cockroaches crowded the ground. You had to stomp your feet so they would scatter away and give you room to squat. But, as soon as your feet were set in place, the cockroaches would return and crawl over your shoes.

On that very first morning, I turned away from the latrine in disgust. As I did so, I noticed children's heads peering at us from behind the trees. Some children snuck up to us, but none of them would come closer than a few metres. Jane and I were the first white people to enter the community and so, for most of the children, we were ghosts. The kids had seemed fine the night before, but perhaps that was because Andrew was there and ordering them around. With him gone, they seemed both curious and anxious.

One of the young girls was rocking from side to side on the tips of her toes. When I waved, she leant back on her heels, looked to the ground and erupted into giggles. Her laughter had a hint of cheekiness and was full of life. I later learnt that her name was Victoria; this first encounter was the start of a great friendship.

Standing just behind Victoria was a younger girl, Mirimu, wearing a torn navy dress. She would have only been a few years old, and she stared wide-eyed at me. I took a few steps closer to her and her jaw dropped—she began howling with fear. Victoria tried to comfort her and lead her away, but Mirimu was so terrified that her body was frozen still. I felt guilty. I wanted to pick her up and comfort her, but I didn't want to make things worse so I walked back to the front of our house.

Across the road a boy was playing with a small grass-woven ball. As he kicked it about, I caught him glancing over at me. We exchanged a smile. Then Andrew appeared; his smile seemed to have widened overnight. He greeted us, and asked us how the night was. We all replied that we had slept well.

I had noticed that everyone in the community—Andrew and the children included—had a shaved head. I asked him about this and he told me that it was to prevent headlice. *Headlice?* I was shocked. In Australia, I had heard on the news about famines and the AIDS epidemic and civil wars. But what was truly devastating about now being face-to-face with poverty was that even the smallest things—things we wouldn't even think about in Australia—were problems.

Andrew offered to show us to the borehole. He had brought us an extra jerry can so we now had two 20-litre ones. Lillian and Wemusa decided to wait at the house, while Jane and I were eager to learn how to collect water. We followed Andrew behind our house and down a little dirt path, winding between crops, bushes and trees. We passed children coming back up the path. The jerry cans were larger than the children themselves, and they dragged them along the ground between their legs, water splashing out against their legs as they walked.

When we reached the borehole, there were many women and children gathered around, waiting for their turn. Again we attracted many stares, and a few children stumbled backwards while watching us cautiously. Andrew greeted everyone as if they were old friends, but he didn't actually know them because he lived further down the road and this wasn't the borehole he usually used.

A small boy was filling his jerry can. The pump obviously required all of his strength, as the boy was jumping up and then using all of his bodyweight to pull it down. Water flowed out, some going into the can and some splashing onto the surrounding dirt. When the can was full, he heaved it along the ground to one of the women waiting. It wasn't his jerry can, after all. Next he grabbed a can from one of the other women and began the whole process again.

I watched in amazement. After a while, the boy came to fill our jerry cans, but Jane and I said that we could do it ourselves. We lined the can up, and then took it in turns to pull the pump down. It was quite heavy but it was also fun. Those standing by shared a laugh with us at our weakness and lack of technique. A few of the women and children gestured us to move to the side, as they demonstrated how we should do it. We needed to put a little back into it!

Filling the can turned out to be the easy part. When Jane and I each tried to lift one, it was unbelievably difficult. I could only carry the can about 3 metres and then I needed to put it down, rest and swap hands. Andrew found it difficult to watch us struggling and wanted to help, but Jane and I were both a little stubborn. Finally we compromised by letting Andrew carry one of the cans. We put a stick through the handle of the other, took either side, and slowly hauled it back to the house.

Once we got there and had put the cans inside, Andrew suggested we walk to the trading centre to buy a charcoal stove and mozzie nets. He had to return to the primary school to teach but he pointed down the road, advising us where to go.

The trading centre was about 2 kilometres away, and a delightful walk. It was a hot day and the ground had already dried from the downpour the night before. We walked slowly. Lillian did not like walking as the high heels that she wore sunk into the dirt with every step. Like Wemusa, she dressed quite formally or, as it was described in Uganda, 'she looked smart'.

Clothes seemed to be a bit strange here: people always dressed at either end of the spectrum, either in little or tattered clothing, or in formal dress. It was as though everyone just wore whatever they could find until they could afford to buy a nice pair of pants and collared shirt for the men or the traditional dress for the women (*gomesi*). While the women wore their brightly coloured *gomesis* with pride, they had to be one of the most impractical pieces of clothing I had ever seen—a full-length dress, with a sash tied around the waist and short puffed sleeves. They were generally made of cotton and might require up to 6 metres of material. How these women wore these outfits and still worked on the land, or walked to the borehole etcetera, amazed me.

The relationship between clothing and status was also interesting. In Namwendwa, it was considered socially inappropriate for women to wear pants and there was also a widespread belief that women wearing a short skirt were asking to be raped. I wondered how pants related to control and eliteness, as opposed to skirts and dresses. It seemed to be a pretty common concept, not only in Uganda but in Australia too.

As we continued our walk, an elderly woman raced out onto the road, stood in front of us and reached out towards us. She shook both my hands at once, and then moved on to shake the hands of the others as well. She was a tiny woman—skin and bone, and no taller than four foot five. Her head nodded with joy as she shook our hands. The woman gestured us over to her home, welcoming us in the local language. English is the official language in Uganda, but each of the rural areas has its own dialect. In Namwendwa, this was Lusoga. Most elderly people in the village, and all of the children, only spoke Lusoga. Only those who had the chance to go to school were able to speak some English. When children started primary school they were taught in Lusoga and then slowly more English was used as they progressed up through the year levels. They had to sit for all their exams in English. This was one of many reasons why those who were schooled in rural areas were disadvantaged—they were learning in their second language. Lillian was from a nearby area, so she understood Lusoga, but Wemusa's family was from a completely different region, so the language was as new to him as it was to Jane and me.

When we reached the old woman's home, a mud hut, there were many elders sitting outside, the women on woven mats and the men on wooden chairs. They each greeted us, shaking our hands, thrilled to have our company. The woman who had invited us over raced inside and returned with two wooden chairs. She smiled, and nodded again, wanting us to sit. I chose to sit on the mat instead, firstly because I actually preferred the mat, but also because that's where the other women were seated. I had already noticed that being white seemed to give me the same status as men, and it made me feel uncomfortable.

All the older people were nodding and smiling as we sat there. I felt a bit useless with my extremely limited Lusoga, and our hostess didn't seem to know what to do with herself once we were seated. She raced inside again and this time she returned carrying a book and a pencil. She handed us the book. It seemed to be a very strange book for her to hand to us, but I later learnt that such guest books are actually treasured possessions for Ugandans. I took the pencil and filled it out.

Name	Date	Comment
Nikki Lovell	31/02/2005	Beautiful country. Thanks for making us so welcome.

5
Bad News

NAMWENDWA, UGANDA, March 2005

I'm not religious, but nevertheless I was in church. It had been assumed that I was Christian and so, wanting to be accepted and respected within the village, I had taken up Andrew's offer to take us to the Sunday morning service. Lillian and Jane were with me. Wemusa had stayed home, which was a little bit ironic, given that he actually was Christian.

The church was a single-room mud-brick building, on the primary school grounds. All the women were dressed in their most beautiful *gomesi*. The service was in Lusoga, so I didn't understand much of what was said. At one point a basket was handed around and people placed items in it, such as small bags of rice or eggs. Then, to my surprise, the service turned into an auction. It was a hoot! Everyone ended up with some food to take home later—we bought a pineapple—and the church got cash. I really liked this system and was beginning to feel comfortable, but then the priest summoned Lillian, Jane and me up the front. As newcomers to the village, he asked us to introduce ourselves. In very basic Lusoga, I said a few words. I felt like such a *munzungu*, but everyone still clapped and cheered.

After the service, we walked home. Andrew and Jane were chatting and I was with Lillian. An elderly man approached me, speaking in Lusoga. He was holding his arm out to me while nodding. I looked to Lillian questioningly, and she said the man wanted me to rub his arm. It was an extremely strange request, but I thought maybe it was a village greeting or something, so I did as the man asked. It was a little bit uncomfortable, but afterwards the man nodded even more enthusiastically and was smiling, so I assumed I had done the right thing.

Once he had left, I asked Lillian about it. She told me that the man had wanted to prove to me that he wasn't black because he was dirty. I was shocked and embarrassed that he thought I would believe such a thing and realised that some people must have thought I was seeing black skin for the first time.

There were moments such as this one where I felt overwhelmed by simple daily encounters. Then there were others when I felt detached and bored. This was how it was at Namwendwa Primary School. It was a government school with over 1000 students, with class sizes exceeding 100 and most classes with no furniture, so the kids just sat on the ground. We were supposed to be teaching health, but the school had not yet included our classes in the curriculum. So, instead of teaching life-saving information, I was spending countless hours just hanging about in the school staff room and wishing time away. It was ridiculous and frustrating.

The 'staff room' was in fact a mango tree that all the teachers sat under. I was grateful to be outside, but still felt tense. I had spent many days under this tree by now and had already been introduced to all the teachers multiple times. But their names were different to the sort of names I was used to—names like 'Cosmos'—and I found it impossible to remember them and so I was left feeling uncomfortable and rude, often hiding away behind a book.

Lillian fitted in so beautifully. Not only did she speak Lusoga and know this area, but she was also a qualified teacher. Everyone loved her. Jane too, seemed to slide easily into this picture. She was so friendly and open; she also had a knack for remembering names and Lusoga words. She picked things up quickly, while I sunk further into my chair.

Wemusa spent most days lying on his bed. He wasn't interested in coming to the school until the curriculum was organised. And in those moments when I felt so utterly out of place, I consoled myself that at least I fitted in more than Wemusa. Pathetic, I know.

The other problem with having nothing to do was that I had way too much time to think. It amazed me (and not in a pleasing way) how I could have the same stream of thoughts again and again and again. I was constantly thinking of Jack—well, not so much of him but of my need to end things. And then I was thinking about Luke. I didn't really know what to think of this whole situation, but that just made me think about it all the more.

My thoughts were circular and frustrating. Then my frustration would turn to irritation as I would feel annoyed at myself for not being swept up by the experience of just being in Namwendwa, a place so beautiful and unique. For years I had been craving this adventure, this opportunity to be of use; but now that I was here, I almost didn't feel like I was here at all. I was stuck in my head.

On this particular afternoon, Lillian was chatting with one of the male teachers, Jane was cradling one of the teacher's babies, and I had my nose buried in *The Da Vinci Code*. I was reading the same page for the third time when the primary school headmaster started strutting toward us. *What was his name?! Damn it—think, brain!*

'Good morning, Sam!' Jane perked up.

Sam! That was it. It actually was a common name—the name of one of my brothers, for crying out loud—but I *still* kept forgetting it. Hopeless.

Sam greeted us enthusiastically. He was a boisterous character, full of energy, and he loved the sound of his own voice. The shape of his face reminded me of a hippopotamus and he had a long wide nose. I had liked him immediately. He was easy to be around because he always led a conversation or situation and I could just go with the flow. Now he had strutted over in time to join us for lunch. Each day the school cook would serve us each a large spoonful of *porcho* and a few beans. The *porcho* was made out of ground maize that had been boiled into a hard mush. It made me think of play-dough—a sort of flavourless gunk. We ate it with our hands. Afterwards I always imagined the *porcho* sitting in the pit of my stomach—it felt like it might stay in there forever.

After lunch, Sam stood up in front of me. Then he blurted out that I was going to be 'soooooooooo fat' by the time I left Uganda. *What?!* It was a good job that I had finished swallowing, or I may have spat my *porcho* right back out. Sam went on to say that I was big-boned and then he began to enact just how fat he envisaged me becoming. He held his arms out to his sides and then wobbled about like a sumo wrestler. He wasn't trying to insult me—in Uganda being fat was a privilege. But I wasn't Ugandan, and I didn't want to be fat.

Everyone was laughing. Andrew joined in the sumo-wrestler/my-future enactment, and I tried really hard to smile. Back when we were training, Ugandan honesty had seemed refreshing, but at that time it hadn't been directed at me.

Jane was probably one of the thinnest people I had ever seen. She had an incredible figure—insanely thin and yet she still had big boobs. How does that even happen?

All the attention was focused on me, even though I only weighed 50 kilograms and never before in my life had been called fat—at least, not to my face. I had wanted to be drawn into the moment—for my mind to be totally in the now—but this wasn't what I had in mind. I felt like crap. I wanted to run away. I wanted Luke to wrap me in his arms and tell me I was beautiful. But I had nowhere to run to, and Luke was not here. So instead I sat still, and concentrated on smiling and not crying. I was relieved when those teachers who were actually included in the school curriculum retreated to their classrooms and all the Nikki Being Fat talk subsided.

After too many days of waiting for the primary and secondary schools to get their act together with their curriculums, we realised we could be waiting for months. So we decided to watch the classrooms and when there seemed to be no teacher present, we would conduct a lesson until a teacher showed up. We would divide into pairs for each lesson. For my very first lesson, I was with Lillian in the primary school, while Jane and Wemusa were in the secondary school. In most classes kids sat on the ground, but in this room there were wooden benches with thin blocks of wood that served as desks. The kids squashed against each other so they could all have a seat. Some bottoms hung off the edges of the benches, but the kids didn't seem fazed.

The purpose of our first lesson was to introduce ourselves, to introduce health broadly—it had never been taught in Namwendwa before—and to begin to establish relationships with the kids. I spoke first, beginning nervously and then growing in confidence as the kids seemed to be hanging off my every word. When I finished my little introduction, I had a big grin, feeling proud. The kids had more than a grin—they simply burst into laughter. They had been trying to control their giggles the entire time I had been speaking, but now they couldn't help themselves. Apparently they hadn't understood a word I had said! Their English was still very basic and to them my accent just sounded like someone putting on a funny voice. I tried to introduce myself again in my very basic Lusoga, but evidently this was even funnier.

I was just as useless inside the classroom as I had been sitting under the mango tree reading my book. Lillian calmed the class down and completed the lesson in Lusoga. I stood in the corner and wondered what on earth I was going to do for the next seven months.

Life at home was no easier than at school. Cooking every night was a time-consuming task. First we would need to break up the pieces of charcoal, throwing them against the ground and then collecting the smaller pieces to put in our charcoal stove. The stove was a small metal contraption—the coals went underneath, and above them was a wire grid to place a pot on for cooking. We would scrunch up some scraps of paper and push them in between the bits of charcoal. Then we would light the paper, blow on it gently and beg for the coals to catch alight.

While this was happening, we would pour some brown peas on a plate, sorting the peas from stones, or bits of stick. Next the peas would need to be rinsed. Then a pot of water would be placed on the stove and, once it was boiling, in would go the peas. They would take hours to cook, and the whole time you needed to keep an eye on the charcoal, making sure it stayed alight. When the peas were ready, this whole process would need to be repeated to cook some rice.

Given that it took so long, we decided to take it in turns to prepare the meal each night. I liked this system—it forced me to be independent, and I enjoyed trying to be creative with very limited ingredients. Jane and Lillian also quite enjoyed cooking, and Lillian was an excellent cook. Wemusa was the only one who didn't like the system. After one of us had cooked his dinner, he would leave his meal sitting there uneaten for an hour or so. He would never say thank you, and his lack of any gratitude was hurtful. Later he would pick at the food, pushing it around his bowl, unimpressed. Then he would leave his dirty bowl, expecting us to clean up after him. On his nights to cook, Wemusa would disappear. If we waited for him, we would go hungry. He would return home late, cook himself some rice, and then leave the pot unwashed as well as his bowl littered with scraps.

Wemusa was tall and bony and didn't seem to require that much food. His complete lack of respect for us was more than hurtful; it was bloody annoying. It wasn't just the cooking or cleaning either. He also wouldn't fetch water or prepare lesson plans. I could understand why he was the way he was—his dad had multiple wives and he had over 30 siblings, more than he could recall by name. In his world, women did everything and men were always right. But understanding his background didn't make the situation any less aggravating. I also felt a little used. Being an international volunteer, I had paid the organisation a significant donation so that they could supplement the Ugandan volunteers' living expenses. I felt that working alongside the Ugandan volunteers was a critical part of the program. I could learn a lot from Lillian and Wemusa, but I felt it should have been a two-way process and it bothered me that Wemusa was not even open to consider that there may be other ways to live.

Neither Jane nor Lillian said much to Wemusa, not wanting to make matters worse. I was stupid and thought maybe we could just talk things through. However, Lillian and Jane were right—any of my attempts to talk with Wemusa just created further tension within the house. He would sit silently and give me death stares. His dark eyes seemed to drill through me, and I would sit looking back at him. I was stubborn, like my dad; but all the while, I knew I was facing a losing battle. Eventually I would give up, and retire to Jane's and my room. We had been given beds now, and Lillian had moved into the main room. Jane's and my beds only just fitted into the room, with about 5 centimetres between them.

It wasn't just Wemusa and my lack of teaching success giving me discomfort; I was also constipated. Thinking I needed to go, I would grab the toilet paper and dash to the latrine. But as I approached, the stench would become overwhelming. When I swung the wooden door open, the flies would suddenly be swarming around me. There were the signs of diarrhoea everywhere. Holding my nose, I would place my feet either side of the hole, my sandals squashing the muddy shitty mixture. I held the toilet paper in my mouth so I could hoist my skirt up. The flies would be buzzing around my ankles. It was unbearable. Any need to go to the toilet disappeared almost instantaneously. I would sigh as I left the stinky latrine.

Later that night, when the need re-emerged I would consider ducking behind a bush but there seemed to be people everywhere. I would prepare to squat and then hear giggles from above. I would look up and there would be kids perched in the tree. Even in the dark it was an impossible mission, as being white I glowed. Being white also meant that eyes followed me with curiosity wherever I went.

One night I felt really bloated and disgusting but wondered whether I was just making excuses and was actually getting fat. As I sat on my bed, I felt I needed some distraction from everything. Jane was outside cooking, so I had a brief moment of privacy. I started searching through my backpack. Everything I used I had already pulled out and had hanging in bags from nails on the wall beside my bed. A few random bits and pieces remained in my pack. I pulled out a small black bag, and opened it to find syringes and little boxes of various pills—my medical kit. Dad, being a doctor, had put it together for me and this was the first time I had looked through it. I emptied the bag's contents onto my bed and examined the different boxes. Dad had also typed up a list of everything in the bag and laminated it (though I suspected the laminating was Mum's touch). At the bottom of the list Dad had written: 'Most importantly remember we love you and are thinking of you. Love Dad.'

It wasn't the sort of thing that Dad would normally say to me, but it was exactly what I needed. I found myself hugging the piece of paper, tears flowing. Good job it was laminated. Even though such emotion was rare for Dad to show, the note still reminded me of my life before all this—before awkward language barriers, standing out like a ghost, shit-covered long drops, men with little respect for women. But the note also brought me back to a life that was just as uncomfortable, yet in different ways. A life where I had every reason to be happy, but I hadn't been. I had been restless and uneasy with the world. I struggled as much there as I did here, and there was something both unsettling and reassuring in that.

I was still clutching the paper when Jane came to the doorway to announce that dinner was ready. She noticed my watery eyes and the tears smudged on my cheeks and asked if I was okay. I smiled and said I would explain later. As I followed her outside to eat, I realised it was only the two of us. Wemusa was probably meandering about in the trading centre, but Lillian's whereabouts were a mystery. Jane and I had gone to the borehole earlier in the day; when we had returned, she was gone. We had assumed that she was just at one of the schools, but it was strange for her to still not be home.

The next morning I got up early to wash, and noticed that Lillian's bed was still empty. Perhaps she had arrived home late, and was already up and about this morning. I was trying to be positive. I had my towel and bed sheet slung over my shoulder, and my toiletries bag in my hand. I put my bag down and filled the yellow basin with water from one of our jerry cans. Then I put my bag in my mouth, freeing my hands to carry the full basin out to the bathing area.

Many people had obviously already washed as the bricks of the bathing area were saturated with soapy water. I crept in and put my basin down. Then I wandered back out and found some heavy stones. I hung my sheet up, using stones to weigh it down on either side of the gap between the two top bricks. My makeshift door was as much privacy as I was going to get.

Even though it was still early, the sun's heat was already intense and I was grateful for that. I undressed slowly, my eyes watching my sheet with caution. I placed my towel and clothes over one of the brick walls to keep them dry. Then I pulled some soap out of my toiletries bag and stood in the basin, splashing the water onto myself. It was difficult to wash properly with only a small basin of water, but being outside was relaxing. I loved the feeling of the sun shining on me as I scrubbed the dirt out of my skin. I imagined myself getting a perfect tan and smiled at the thought.

But just as I was at peace, a forceful gust of wind blew and lifted my sheet up. The stones were still in place, so it only flew into the air for a moment but it was as if it all happened in slow motion. The bathing area was behind our house, and just in front of our house was the dusty road that led to both the primary and secondary schools. At the exact time that my sheet floated up, secondary school students were walking down the road and they caught a glimpse of my white naked body. *Oh god!* I was going to be teaching these students and *this* was our first encounter. I quickly grabbed at my towel, dried myself and got dressed again.

Jane was dressed and boiling water for tea when I entered the house. We assumed Wemusa was still in bed. We had a quick cuppa and decided to walk to the schools to see if anyone had seen Lillian. I was reluctant to go to the secondary school following my earlier embarrassment, so I offered to ask around at the primary school instead.

The teachers had not seen Lillian but reassured me not to worry. Then they asked if I would teach. I felt panicked. The thought of teaching on my own was more than daunting; it seemed impossible. But I couldn't say no. I entered the class, and 100 or more students in pink uniforms looked up at me. Who would have thought a room full of little kids dressed in pink could be so intimidating.

This was a different class than Lillian and I had taught last time, so they didn't know who I was. I introduced myself slowly in English, and then I asked in Lusoga if they understood me. They nodded and smiled. I didn't want to just talk at the kids, so I decided to teach them a song. At the training we had learnt a song called 'Under the mango tree'. I really liked it, as you could act out every line—it was good fun. I gestured for all the kids to stand up, and then I started singing and acting out the song. At first the kids just looked at each other, in part amusement and part confusion; but, as I continued, they started to join in.

This was the first time I had ever sung in public. I have a terrible, terrible singing voice and am well aware of it, but the kids didn't seem to care. When we were singing together and moving our arms like the swaying leaves of the mango tree, it was magic. I was so exposed, being completely myself, dreadful singing voice and all—and it was bliss. The kids cheered when we finished the song and I left the class with a smile. I hadn't even mentioned the syllabus or taught them anything to do with health, but that would come later.

That afternoon Lillian was still missing. Wemusa seemed content, simply lying on his bed, so Jane and I decided to catch a *matatu* from the trading centre to the nearest town, Kamuli. The driver was an absolute nutter, no exaggerating. As we raced along the dusty road, he would press his hand down firmly on his horn. This was a painfully loud and alarming warning signal: 'Get out of my way *NOW!*' As we sped on, a *buda-buda* man who had been coming toward us screamed as he frantically swerved to miss the blue blur of our *matatu*. I swung my head around to search for the *buda-buda* man but instead got an eyeful of dirt as it flew in through the small gap where the window had been pushed open.

Kamuli was a small dusty town and the *matatu* station was at its hub. There were probably at least 15 *matatu*s either coming or going at any time. The town had a bustling feel with people hassling you the moment you stepped out of the *matatu*. You would find yourself encircled by *buda-buda* men, while others would just call out in amusement, '*Munzungu, munzungu!*' Even in this little town, being white was a novelty. This was not the sort of place that attracted tourists. The dirt streets were littered with little shops on either side. Most were clothes stalls, selling the colourful material that the women would buy to make their *gomesi*. There were also trading shops, with tins of paint and various tools. It amazed me that all the shops survived, given that there seemed to be little difference from one to the next.

Other than the shops, there was also a bank that always had queues going out the door and along the street. There

The road to Namwendwa, Uganda where I lived and worked. I loved walking down this track with the lush green surroundings—so, so beautiful. *One Village collection*

Families working on their land. What you grow is what you eat. *One Village collection*

Cattle on the move. *Photo courtesy of Lisa Duffy*

What are you looking at? *Photo courtesy of Lisa Duffy*

Local homes in Namwendwa. It's amazing how many people may live in a single mud hut. *One Village collection*

Ugandan family: Wemusa, Lillian, Jane and myself proudly wearing hats that the community made for us. *One Village collection*

Community borehole where everyone collects their water. Young children would walk home dragging the heavy jerry cans between their legs. *One Village collection*

At the borehole closest to our home. We would use this 20-litre jerry can of water to drink, cook, wash ourselves and wash all our dishes. *Photo courtesy of Jane Barett*

Florence and me in the Infant School (bamboo building). *Photo courtesy of Jane Barett*

The Infant School (2005) where adorable children welcomed me in song. *One Village collection*

Jinja markets; well worth the maze through the mud. *One Village collection*

The markets are a place of spicy delight. *One Village collection*

The best way to get around town. *'Mangu, mangu!'* means 'quick, quick' in the local dialect, Lusoga. You can see why I picked the red bike! *Photo courtesy of Lisa Duffy*

Cattle trucks are often also used as buses and are probably more comfortable! *One Village collection*

Kampala, Uganda's capital. The city is set over ten hills and its name is derived from the Kiganda expression 'kasozi k'empala' (the hills of antelopes), but it still just felt like a big, dirty city to me. *One Village collection*

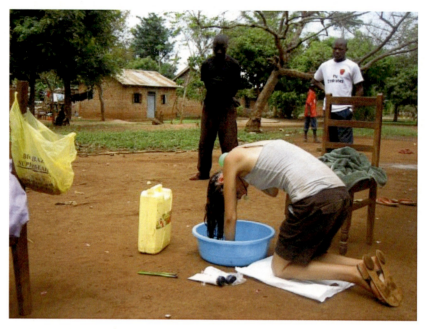

Washing my hair gains spectators. Most people in the community have shaved heads to prevent the spread of headlice. *One Village collection*

The photo of my little brother, Josh, that I took with me to Namwendwa. Even in print his smile is contagious.

were two small supermarkets as well where you could buy bread, spaghetti, various jars of things, and sometimes milk or liquid yoghurt. Almost all of the shops and the supermarkets were owned by Indians. This was also the case with the small shops in Namwendwa trading centre. I made a mental note to learn more about Uganda's history.

The town didn't have the majestic feel of the village, but it was useful for picking up a few supplies that made life in Namwendwa slightly more comfortable. Kamuli also had phone reception. I had a mobile with me, but hadn't used it yet. I still needed a Ugandan SIM card. I popped into the supermarket and was able to buy one. I had Luke's number saved to my phone, even though I had never had a use for it until now. My heart was beating so fast and loud, it felt as if it might pop right out of me. I told myself that Luke and I were just friends and I had no reason to feel so strange about calling him. Then I swallowed my nerves.

Luke was surprised to hear my voice and I was surprised to hear that he was in Jinja, a long way from the village where he was supposed to be. He offered to come and visit me in Namwendwa and, perhaps a little too enthusiastically, I said that was a great idea. I would meet him in Kamuli in a few days' time.

The large marketplace was the other highlight of Kamuli. Just next to the *matatu* station, it was a maze of little stalls selling fresh fruit and vegetables. Heaven! We meandered through and were happy to pick up some carrots, capsicums, tomatoes, potatoes, onions and even garlic. We bartered with stall owners to buy a pineapple but everyone was intent on charging us three times the local price. Grrrr! We didn't want to start a precedent of paying more, so we left the markets with just our vegetables.

As we went to clamber back onto the *matatu*, we spotted another man selling pineapples. He had them tied all around his bicycle and was standing peacefully on the outskirts of the *matatu* station. We raced over, greeted him in Lusoga and asked him how much. This man had a gentle nature, and he lifted the different-sized pineapples, quoting their prices—all local prices. We smiled and got the biggest pineapple he had.

Back in Namwendwa, on the walk home from the trading centre, we were bouncing with joy as we discussed the vegetable spaghetti we planned to make that night. It was the first time that we were going to have vegies in a long time and we were super excited. Admittedly I was also thinking about Luke, having no idea what to expect when I saw him, but knowing that I was seriously looking forward to it.

Halfway home we were startled as SPW's red 4WD raced past. An unexpected visit? The vehicle screeched to a stop—we had obviously been spotted. Jane and I approached the driver's window to come face-to-face with a bewildered Charles. He didn't have his usual goofy grin. He didn't get out of the car, or even bother with greeting us. Instead he just stared directly at us. Finally he spoke. 'I have some bad news.'

6
A Kiss and a Kill

NAMWENDWA, UGANDA, April 2005

'Your grandmother has passed away,' Charles said bluntly.

He was staring at Jane. I stood helplessly as my friend erupted into tears beside me. I could not believe, nor comprehend what was happening. Things can change in just a blink. We climbed into the car and Charles drove us back to Kamuli so Jane could call her family.

That night we didn't cook vegetable spaghetti. I didn't know what to say or do because at that moment there wasn't anything that could make Jane's pain go away. Wemusa stayed hidden in his room, and Lillian was still missing. Our house was full of silence and sadness.

The next morning Jane and I again took a *matatu* to Kamuli. Our intention was no longer searching for fresh ingredients but simply that Jane could speak to her family again. I tried to give her space as she spoke on the phone. An elderly woman approached me and asked why my *munzungu* friend was so tearful. I didn't have enough Lusoga to explain the situation, but emotions seem to transcend words and the friendly stranger nodded in understanding.

I glanced towards Jane and noticed that she seemed to be swaying. My heart skipped a beat as I saw the phone slip from her hand and fall to the ground. I raced over to her as she fainted, reaching her just in time to stop her head hitting the ground. Cradling Jane's head in my arms, I felt completely overwhelmed. I had no idea what to do, but fortunately locals came and assisted me. I was so grateful as they helped me lie her down. She was just lying there... Not moving. Eyes closed. She looked dead and it terrified me. I knelt next to her, squeezing her hand and praying to a God I didn't believe in. What felt like an eternity later, Jane opened her eyes and spoke. I cannot describe the relief.

Back at Namwendwa later that day, Jane told me that she was considering going back to England for the funeral. Her only hesitation was her fear that if she was reunited with her family and boyfriend, it would be too difficult to say goodbye yet again and return to Uganda.

Despite only having been in Uganda just over a month, I couldn't imagine returning to Australia. My family would have moved to Ireland by now and strangers would be living in the house I grew up in. Most of my friends were also overseas, having their own adventures. Jack would be there, but I wouldn't want to see him. Such thoughts had been lingering in my head since I arrived, but I now realised quite intensely not just that I felt disconnected to Australia but that there literally was nothing left for me to return to. It was almost unbelievable that the building blocks of my existence for the past 18 years seemed to have fallen apart so abruptly.

Jane and I were talking in our room when the missing Lillian reappeared. She looked completely fine but had a sly smile, as though she was hiding something. We were both relieved and surprised to see her, and asked where on earth she had been. She was hesitant in answering, shuffling about on her feet. Then she came and sat on Jane's bed. The three of us were so close to each other in that tiny room. Lillian looked through the small space between Jane's and my beds, her eyes fixed on the ground. She obviously didn't want to tell us where she had been and maybe we didn't need to know. She was back now and that was all that mattered. Instead Jane told Lillian her own news and Lillian comforted her.

With everything that was going on, my embarrassment about my flying-sheet bathing experience seemed insignificant so I braved up and decided to teach a lesson in the secondary school. It was strange teaching there because most of the students were physically larger than me. Many of them may have been older than me too, given that most people only went to school when they could afford it.

Uganda had a Universal Primary Education Program, so primary school was free for up to four children from each Ugandan family. It was still not compulsory, but the government's goal was to provide every Ugandan child with the opportunity for a primary school education. Broadly, the program seemed to be achieving its goal. As always, though, there were a few exceptions. For instance, although the school fees were provided, wearing a school uniform was compulsory and it needed to be purchased by the child's family. It was less than $20 for a uniform, but for some families even this was too much.

I was also not sure how the term 'family' was defined, since many children shared only the same mother or father. I was quite taken aback when I first met some of the kids and they were explaining their families. They would say, 'This is Sara, same mother, different father. This is Nasa, same father, different mother.' Polygamy was normal here. It was also legal, which surprised me given that Uganda was predominately a Christian nation.

Unlike primary school, secondary school was not government funded. School fees, uniform and all supplies only cost about $130 in total, but that was a large amount to pay if your only income was from selling a few tomatoes outside your home. Given this, it seemed that less than 25 per cent of students had the opportunity to go onto secondary school and I noticed immediately how most students were male. Females were often kept at home—to work on the land or help out around the house—or else they entered into an early marriage.

The classrooms were better equipped than at the primary school. They were still brick buildings with open spaces for the doors and windows, and dirt floors and tin roofs, but every classroom had a blackboard and sufficient wooden benches for the students to sit on. I discovered that writing on the blackboard was actually quite difficult and my handwriting looked somewhat like a five-year-old's. I felt quite intimidated standing up at the front of the room; as an 18-year-old white girl with only three weeks' training on health material and teaching techniques, who was I to now teach these kids anything of use? I also felt unsure because I had planned to speak about menstruation. But now, realising how many males were in the class, I wondered whether I should be teaching something else instead.

I took a deep breath and stopped that train of negative thoughts. *I am a female*, I told myself, and I thought how grateful I was that I'd learnt at school all about having my period. I turned to look at the girls in the room; there were probably about 15 of them out of the class of 50 or more students. I imagined their fear when they had first bled. The SPW staff had told us at our training that the girls would do all sorts of things in an effort to stop the bleeding, including trying to stuff a small eggplant up themselves. *An eggplant!*

Suddenly I felt confidence flowing through me and I began. After the explanatory part of the class, I taught the students practical things to help the girls cope with their period. I addressed three main issues. The first was coping with period pain, and I showed them some simple stretches that may help. I then talked about making a calendar to track their periods so it was easier for them to be prepared. Finally I spoke about what to use and not to use during their period. It was not possible to buy pads in Namwendwa, and it was not possible to buy tampons anywhere in the country. However, we had been shown at our training how to make a pad out of a square piece of cotton fabric and a slip of cellophane or plastic bag. I demonstrated making a pad like this, and all the students watched inquisitively.

After forty minutes, I left the class feeling that my time with those girls may actually have been extremely useful for them and would make their lives slightly more comfortable. *I can be of use*, I smiled to myself as I walked back home.

●

Jane decided to stay in Uganda—she planned to say goodbye to her grandma in her own way. Selfishly, I was happy and relieved that she would not be leaving; she was the glue that held our household together. I wasn't particularly good about being empathetic toward Wemusa's behaviour but, with Jane there too, I felt calm enough to limit my number of arguments with him.

Jane was staying but Lillian was gone . . . again. This time we were not worried or concerned but annoyed. If she was going to make a habit of disappearing it would be nice at least to have a little warning about when she was going and when she would be back. But I didn't have time to be too annoyed for I too had places to be. I was to meet Luke in Kamuli and that afternoon he was going to come back to Namwendwa with me for a little visit. When Luke and I had said goodbye, I hadn't anticipated seeing him again so soon. We had left things in an unusual way—we had been very close to transcending the barrier between friendship and something more. But we hadn't quite crossed it, and neither of us had said anything about the change in our relationship. The way we had been together had just felt natural and the need to define it would have spoiled the moment. But of course now I had no clarity as to what was what.

    I stopped pacing outside the petrol station and sat down. *Stop thinking about how you are supposed to be and just be,* I told myself. I took a deep breath and, when I looked up, there was Luke. He had a large grin on his face and a small block of chocolate in his hand.

    We caught a *matatu* back to Namwendwa and chatted on the walk to my house. We both had a lot of stories to swap, despite having been apart for just a short time. When we reached my place, we went to Jane's and my room. Jane was sitting on her bed reading, but she put her book down when we entered. Luke and I sat on my bed, and we talked about the week that had been. While we were chatting, I lay down and rested my head on his lap. He played with my hair and stroked my arm. Jane was struggling to control her grin.

    There was an obvious change in the air. Jane must have felt it too because she made an excuse to leave the room. Then Luke lay down and took my hands in his own. We didn't say anything—we just lay there, looking at each other with big goofy smiles.

The mood was slightly put on hold by dinner. For dessert, we bought some *chapattis* and then melted Luke's chocolate onto them. Having chocolate was an absolute treat and melting it was Jane's ingenious idea. It was *amazing!* After such indulgence, I felt more than a little bloated and went to lie down. Luke followed me back into the bedroom while Jane stayed in the main room. Things took off exactly where they had left off. I was happy but my curiosity was starting to get the better of me, and so I couldn't help asking Luke how he felt about me. He responded sarcastically, telling me he thought I was fat and ugly. I punched him flirtatiously and asked for a serious answer. He told me that he didn't act like this with his other female friends, and so that sort of showed how he felt about me.

I replied that I was confused because of Sarah, his girlfriend. He told me that he was equally confused because of Jack. I didn't want Luke to feel any pressure to do or say anything but I told him that being in Uganda had made me realise that my feelings for Jack weren't as I had thought and that I had decided to end the relationship. Luke said he felt the same about Sarah.

I was unsure what should happen next. After all, we had both just admitted to having feelings for each other, but then pointed out that we were both still in other relationships. Where did that leave us? In a literal sense, it left us exactly where we were—two young people, lying on a bed together, enclosed by a mozzie net, so close that our faces were touching. *Shit.*

Luke kissed me lightly on my nose. And then my forehead. And then my cheek . . .

Suddenly a loud thumping at the door interrupted the moment. It was Jane. She popped her head around the doorway, wary of intruding, and said that she was going to sleep in Lillian's bed in the main room. Then she quickly grabbed a few of her things and left, shutting the bedroom door behind her. Jane was a good friend and I felt guilty for making her feel uncomfortable in her own home. But then I was drawn back into the moment with Luke, and I forgot about Jane now sleeping on the other side of the door.

Luke kissed me again on the cheek, and I gave him a light kiss on the tip of his nose. Our lips soon found each other. But after about a minute, I pulled away. *This is wrong*, I thought. And then I said it out loud. I wanted to do the morally right thing, but I also really wanted to kiss Luke again. He was right there, damn it! And his lips were soft and luscious, and so very tempting.

Minutes later, Luke and I kissed again. It was so right and so wrong—both, and at the same time. Things had gone a step further than they had on our final night of the training, but the same internal argument was still going on inside of me. Once again, reason finally won out and I pulled away from Luke with an apologetic expression. Luke seemed to understand and appeared content just lying beside me. Ultimately, he fell asleep, but I didn't. My mind was on overdrive—thinking about what I had done, what I had wanted to do, and wondering what to do next.

When the sun began to rise, I was dreading the thought of having to teach. Jane, the absolute legend, said that she would cover my classes. Presumably she was going to cover

Lillian's and Wemusa's too as their whereabouts were unknown. It felt like déjà vu when it came time for Luke and me to say goodbye. He needed to start the journey back to his own placement. He gave me a quick peck on the lips, and then he was gone.

I had never thought I would be the type of person who would cheat. *Far out.* It had been enough of a surprise to have a boyfriend in the first instance, and Jack had always treated me like a princess. Now this was how I was repaying him. *I am a bad person*, I thought. I told myself that Jack needed to know the truth, but perhaps the reality was that I needed Jack to know the truth. Even when I thought I was about to do the supposedly right thing, if I'm honest, it was more about me than Jack.

I was crying and shaking when I dialled Jack's number. It didn't feel real when I heard his voice. His excitement soon turned to concern for me as my sobbing became increasingly loud. I got straight to the point, telling him that Luke and I had kissed. The line went quiet. I was expecting Jack to shout or cry or something, but instead he was completely calm. He told me that he understood and that he still loved me. *What?!* I hadn't anticipated this. *I didn't want this.* I had assumed that Jack would break up with me when I told him of my betrayal, but now I was going to have to end it.

In that moment I realised that telling someone you don't love them is significantly more difficult than saying you kissed someone else. I might not have loved Jack, but I did still care for him. He had been more than my lover for the last year—he had been my best friend. But now I was going to break his heart.

I told him that I could only be his friend, but he refused to believe it was over. He tried to convince me that it could work, but all I could say was 'no'. I didn't really want to elaborate on my feelings. I just wanted the conversation to be over. I wanted the relationship to be over. I pretended the reception was cutting out, apologised, and hung up.

I spent that night clutching at my stomach as sharp, consistent pain stabbed at me. At about 3 a.m., I quickly pulled my mozzie net off and made a race for a bucket. I sat on the ground in the main room, my legs sprawled on the cold cement floor, my arms wrapped around the bucket and my head hung over it. I remained in this position until light, emptying the contents of my stomach.

I was too tired and sick to teach, so again I stayed home when Jane and Wemusa left to go to the schools. Later I tried to eat some lunch, but I threw that up as well. I wondered whether my body was punishing me for being a bad person. Everyone at the primary school thought that I must be really sick, given that I had missed teaching the other day as well. I felt ashamed that I had just been flirting with a boy. Now everyone was praying for me and hoping that I would have a speedy recovery. Why was everyone being so nice to me? I didn't deserve this.

That evening I started to feel a bit better. Jane, Wemusa and I were sitting on wooden chairs in the main room when in walked the mysterious Lillian. This time we were more persistent in trying to find out what was going on. Lillian sat down on her bed, which was pushed against the back of the main room, and told us that she had a part-time job as a teacher. She had only applied to volunteer with SPW so she would receive the living allowance, which she could then save up. It was shocking to hear that Lillian didn't intend to be on placement very often and that her disappearing acts were going to continue. But what was more distressing was that she had gone to the extreme of being accepted as a volunteer with SPW, just for a few extra dollars a week.

Lillian told us that her mother had passed away, and that she was now trying to look after her younger siblings and save enough money to send them to school. After sharing her story, she looked at us questioningly, wondering whether we were going to tell the SPW staff her secret. Neither Jane nor I would tell them anything, but it was disappointing that Lillian wouldn't be around. We enjoyed her company and she was such a good teacher. But these things paled into insignificance compared to her efforts to send her siblings to school. Wemusa didn't say much, but I doubted he would tell the staff—he liked Lillian too.

That night, it was comforting to know that Lillian, Wemusa and Jane were all there. Although, as it turned out, there weren't just the four of us in the house.

At about 10.15 p.m. all of us were in bed. Wemusa was obviously in a deep sleep as he was making heavy breathing sounds and snoring. Lillian was also presumably asleep. Jane was sitting up in bed, hidden under her mozzie net and writing letters by torchlight. I was in bed wondering why I was not asleep, wishing that I would fall asleep, and worrying that I may not fall asleep at all.

A few moments later a loud crashing sound came from the main room, as though someone was trying to break in. This was followed by a wailing cry. Lillian. She sounded like she had toppled over. As Jane called out to Lillian to see if she was okay, I sat up. When Jane got no response, she jumped out of bed and crept into the main room. She too squealed when she spotted the intruder—a big fat rat.

Mr Ratty was chewing on Lillian's shoe. As Jane started to become a little frantic, I realised I was definitely not going to fall asleep, so I joined the other two girls in the main room. Lillian sat on her bed, while Jane and I both stood a safe distance away from the intruder. The three of us looked at each other. We were all thinking the same thing—*Someone has to kill that rat*. Then, almost in unison, we each said, 'I'm not going to do it!'

As we were wondering who was going to man up and take on the rat, we realised that it had stopped chewing on the shoe. In fact, it appeared to be dead. We watched the rat cautiously—it was now lying on the ground, pink beady eyes staring up at us. Definitely dead. It must have eaten rat poison earlier. Utterly relieved, we decided to retreat to our respective beds. We said we would deal with Mr Rat in the morning, but what we all meant was that Wemusa could deal with the corpse disposal.

Super early next morning, while it was still dark, Jane woke and needed to go to the toilet. Her movement woke me up too. Wemusa was still making his deep sleep noises, and Lillian was awake talking to herself.

Jane rolled out of bed to brave the toilet, but stopped in her tracks when she reached the main room. Mr Ratty was gone! 'Ohhh nooooo!' she cried out.

She quickly dashed to the latrine and, when she returned, she saw the rat scurry into our room. *Great. So now rats can rise from the dead. Isn't that bloody brilliant*, I thought to myself. The rat withdrew to the safety of under my bed. Now I definitely wasn't going to get back to sleep.

Over an hour later the rat still hadn't reappeared, and I was starting to wonder whether it actually had magical powers, and could morph as well as rise from the dead. As if to confirm my suspicions, we then heard the rat in the main room. Wemusa's deep sleep noises had also stopped and so, from the safety of our beds, we called out to Wemusa to come and kill the rat. I realised that we were all being a little bit pathetic and melodramatic but we put up with rats scurrying under our beds every night, and now we felt like we needed a victory.

Wemusa moaned in response but eventually he appeared in the main room. He was only wearing trousers, with bare feet and bare chest, and he held out a long metal stick in front of him. He pounded it against the ground and chanted, 'I am a warrior!'

I nearly wet myself laughing. The rat returned to his favourite position under my bed. Wemusa stormed into our room, threw my sleeping bag and pillow on Jane's bed, and then lifted my mattress onto its side. Between the planks of wood of my bed frame, we could see the rat racing about. Wemusa was trying desperately to poke at it. Jane was jumping up and down on her own bed; I was taking refuge on Lillian's bed; and Lillian, dressed in her nightgown, was guarding the front door to make sure the rat didn't escape.

The rat then made a brave move. He emerged from under my bed and raced into the main room, heading for the open wooden doors and freedom. But Wemusa was on his tail. And then . . . he got him. Wemusa literally prodded the rat to death. I would have felt guilty if I hadn't been so busy being entertained by the armed and near-naked Wemusa. He really did look like a warrior! Later that day, he was still walking around the house chanting 'I am a warrior' and wearing the proudest expression I have ever seen.

This bizarre episode was the closest Wemusa, Lillian, Jane and I had come to bonding so far. We had all shared this hilarious moment, and it had been brilliant. But, just as things started to look up in our house, it all turned to shit—well, technically, it all turned to piss.

I had just started to become confident about using the bathing area again when I went out there one afternoon, basin in my hands, to discover that the area absolutely stunk. It smelt like piss. I looked at the bricks on the ground, and sure enough there was yellow liquid where there should have been soapy water. *Oh god.*

I carried the basin back inside. I stood by the doorway to Jane's and my room and glanced at the space between our beds. There was no way the basin would fit there. I had nowhere to wash. I was about to give up when I decided that I could at least wash my hair. I grabbed my shampoo, comb and a cup and carried the basin to the patch of grass out the front. I knelt on the grass, and dipped my hair into the water in the basin. As I did so, the children from the family across the road came racing over.

I was not only a novelty for being white, but also for my long hair. The children were amused watching me. Victoria had her usual smile; taking the cup from my hands, she scooped it into the basin to fill it with water and then poured it over my head. I noticed that a boy who I often saw playing with a woven ball was also examining me. He stood behind a tree, the ball by his feet, and his eyes followed me with curiosity. I asked Victoria what his name was. 'Dawoodee,' she replied. I realised that he was Victoria's brother, and I guessed he was about 11 years old.

There seemed to be a lot of kids in Victoria's family—eleven children maybe. It was difficult to ask them many questions as their English was as limited as my Lusoga. I learnt who was from which family by watching where they retreated to when the darkness of night crept in.

Jane was absolutely disgusted when she made the same discovery about the bathing area. 'It's a bathing area and a urinal' was Wemusa's reply when she questioned him about it. He didn't seem to understand our concern. I had already had too many confrontations with him so I decided to let

Jane lead this battle. She stormed out to the bathing area, chalk in hand, and wrote on it, 'Bathing only.' I didn't want to say anything but I wasn't sure that was the greatest idea, given that most people in the community understood little English. Jane must have drawn the same conclusion, because later she asked Lillian for a translation and then wrote the note in Lusoga as well. Not that it made any difference—people weren't going to change their habits because of a chalk-written sign.

The next day, we saw Wemusa go in there and urinate. I thought Jane might explode with rage. But she didn't. Instead, she again tried to reason with Wemusa about the hygiene concerns of urinating in the place where we wash ourselves. Wemusa silently sunk into the wooden chair, staring at Jane with a look of death.

I couldn't stand the tension, so I grabbed a skipping rope from my bag and went outside. I hadn't really skipped since primary school but I used to love it. I had thrown a few ropes into my bag before I left Australia; I had thought the kids might enjoy them, but now I actually felt like skipping too.

Skipping was hard work, but I soon started to remember all the tricks that I had perfected as a kid. Everyone marvelled at my skipping even though I must have looked a little ridiculous, jumping high into the air and flinging the rope about my body. The children raced over, laughing, and I handed Kisashi (one of Victoria's older sisters) one of the rope handles. I then held the other handle and we spun the rope, so that the kids could take it in turns to run in and jump.

It was so much fun. The children loved it and it gave me the idea of taking the ropes to the schools. They had no resources for sport, except for space. *I could start a jump rope club*, I thought. I had been captain of our jump rope team at primary school. Of course, I had been eleven then. But now, seven years on, I felt that same enthusiasm buzzing inside of me.

7
Lessons on Love

NAMWENDWA, UGANDA, April 2005

'How do you define love?'

Jane and I were teaching love and relationships in the secondary school. Without set times for when we were to teach, we had the flexibility of teaching lessons individually, in pairs or even as a group. Lillian had already left Namwendwa on this particular morning and Wemusa was teaching in the primary school, so I had the chance to teach with Jane. For this class we had given each student a strip of paper and asked them to write down how they interpreted the word 'love'.

After we'd given the students a few minutes, I collected all the strips and scattered them upside down on the table at the front of the class. Then Jane asked for volunteers to come, randomly pick a piece of paper, and read it out. Hands were thrown into the air; all of them belonged to males. In class, the girls were always so much quieter than the boys. All the behaviour they saw around them told them that men were superior, so naturally they acted as if this must be true.

We selected one of those volunteering to come forward. He almost leaped out of the bench where he was sitting, and practically skipped to the front of the class—he was so excited to be chosen. He picked a piece of paper and read, in English: 'Love is the relationship between a man and a woman.'

We thanked him and invited another student to come forward and do the same. He picked another piece of paper and read: 'Love is the relationship between a man and a woman.'

Huh? We checked the two strips of paper; they did indeed say exactly the same thing.

Another student came forward, and it was like we were on the movie *Groundhog Day*, with the moment repeating itself. Every answer was *exactly* the same. We didn't want to be judgemental, but at the same time we had wanted the students' own thoughts, not a regurgitation of what they had once been told. So we handed out new strips of paper and altered the question slightly: 'What is your meaning of love?' And we banned the definition that they had each given.

'But that's the answer!' they all protested.

Jane explained that we wanted their individual ideas, that there was no right or wrong answer; we just wanted to know how they felt. Eighty blank faces stared up at us.

During my own schooling, I had never realised how often we were asked our own thoughts, opinions and interpretations of things. Even in subjects like science when doing an experiment, there were always questions like, 'What do you think will happen?' and then later, 'Was the result what you expected?'

Developing our own ideas is an integral part of our education system, and it's woven into every aspect of the curriculum. In Uganda, I found myself faced with students who had always been told what to think and who had only ever been talked at—not with. I supposed this was because class sizes were so large and the focus was on the national exam material, as opposed to improving life skills. The result was classes of parrots, who had rote-learned material. They could quote definitions, but didn't actually understand the meaning behind such words.

I had always assumed that the way my brain worked was just part and parcel of who I was; but now I was realising that I had been taught to develop my own ideas and interpretations, which was why I was now in Uganda, rather than at uni. Life was not black and white, nor did I believe it to be a shade of grey. I saw life as a limitless number of colours.

It dawned on me that I shouldn't feel intimidated when teaching, because I didn't need to know every single fact about HIV or malaria or even basic sanitation—all of this could be learnt from a textbook. But a textbook could not teach these kids how they might feel if a loved one or they themselves fell ill; a textbook could not make the boys in this class understand how it felt to be under-valued simply because of being a female. But maybe I could help these students develop their own thoughts, feelings and sense of empathy. At my own school I had learnt about these things through inclusive teaching. Lessons were structured so that there were various levels of difficulty within the set tasks, so that each of us students could participate regardless of our level of ability.

Now I had become a little lost in my thoughts; suddenly I realised the time. Class should have finished five minutes ago. Jane had snuck out of the room early as she was trying to establish a Young Women's Club. Her idea was to facilitate a space where the female students from the school could come together and talk about things that interested them.

I announced the end of class and the students handed in their strips of paper as they left the room. I glanced at the two on top of the pile. The first read: 'Love is the sexing of a girl.' The next read: 'Love is to live on the vagina.'

These students were 16 years old, or older, and I was shocked that this was their understanding of love. Then I thought that perhaps this was unfair of me—perhaps they did have different thoughts and feelings about love as we understand it, but they didn't attach such emotions to that word. Then again, who was I to judge anyone's interpretation of love, given my recent behaviour?

I pushed such thoughts aside and went to the corner of the classroom where my skipping ropes were awaiting me. It was lunchtime, so I decided to test the waters and see if any students showed an interest in a jump rope club. It was just my ropes and me. I looked about outside. At home I had always skipped on asphalt. Here the options were limited to dirt or grass; but skipping on grass was practically impossible, so dirt it was.

I stood on the dirt, threw all the ropes down except one and started skipping. The students all stared at me; some were pointing and laughing. I stopped skipping—this wasn't meant to be entertainment. I held out the rope I had just used, and encouraged some of those staring to give it a try. One girl came forward and told me her name was Harriet. I gave her a rope and she started skipping. She jumped with both feet at once, lifting her knees high; her feet came about half a metre off the ground. Every few jumps, the rope would catch on her feet, but she didn't seem bothered—she simply smiled and tried again.

Four other girls ended up joining in as well. Everyone had to take it in turns as there were only a few ropes, but it was good fun. While only five girls actually participated, there were about 50 onlookers. Perhaps they would join in the next week.

●

While Jane and I had been preparing the lessons on 'love and relationships', I had kept thinking about Luke. I missed him. So much happened every day here and I wanted to be able to share things with him.

Back in Australia, I had never really missed Jack because he was never that far away. I could always pop in the car and visit him; I could call him, email, send him a Facebook message. I always knew that I could reach him almost instantaneously. Here I couldn't even call Luke, because neither of us had phone reception.

Teaching and jump rope had at least temporarily distracted me, but now it was Friday and I had the whole weekend ahead of me. Jane had decided to spend the weekend in Jinja and invited me to join her. It was a tempting offer—some of the other female volunteers would be there, plus Jinja had nice food, internet and phone reception, and the backpackers hostel had a shower (although it was only cold water). But these things didn't seem that great compared to the thought of seeing Luke.

Fuck it, I thought, *I am going to visit Luke!*

I had no idea where the village was that Luke was working in, but I could remember the name of it (at least I hoped I was remembering it correctly). Saturday morning Jane and I caught a *matatu* to Kamuli, where she jumped onto another bus that was going to Jinja. I wished her a lovely weekend and she wished me good luck. I needed it.

I went around to every *matatu* driver, repeating the name of the village where I thought Luke was working. You know you are not doing well at pronouncing something when everyone repeats your words back to you. Each driver pointed me to a different bus, so then I would go and ask that driver. There would be another pause, a confused expression, and then the village name repeated back to me. At which the driver would point somewhere else, and I would repeat the entire process.

I had done two full laps of the *matatu* station and was about to give up hope, when another bus pulled in. I waited for the zillions of passengers, including goats and chickens, to shuffle out and then I went and said the village name to the driver. He tilted his head back and let out a little sigh, which in Uganda seemed to be a common way of saying yes. I said the village name again and, once more, his head went back into the air.

Well, all right then. I clambered into the *matatu*. *Let's see where I end up.*

Being spontaneous felt significantly less exciting when I had to wait over an hour for the bus to fill with enough passengers to satisfy the driver. But finally we were on our way. Once more, being the novelty white girl, everyone wanted to talk to me. No-one cared that my Lusoga was so basic— they were happy that I could say a few words. One young man spoke English and it was as though we were playing the game Twenty Questions. He wanted to know everything. Where was I from? Where in Europe was Australia? Did we all have robots? Were the people in Greenland actually green? His questions were fascinating and it made me wonder what I would have asked if there were a Ugandan on my bus in Australia. But then I thought that I would never have met anyone on the bus in Australia, because I would have purposely sat on my own, deliberately looked out the window, and been listening to my iPod. It bothered me to think that when I returned home I would probably still act in a similar way, because everyone would look at me like I was crazy if I engaged in a conversation with a stranger.

The interesting conversation had made the journey pass quickly and I soon found myself in Luke's village. *Now what?* I still wasn't sure if this was the village where he was working. If it was, I had no idea where his house might be. I must have looked as bewildered as I felt as *buda-buda* men soon called out to me. '*Munzungu, munzungu.*'

That's it! I walked over to the men, hopped on the back of a motorbike and asked them to take me to the other *munzungu*. I figured if this village was anything like Namwendwa, being white would make Luke a celebrity and the *buda-buda* men would know where he lived.

I figured correctly. The *buda-buda* man took me straight to Luke's house. Luke was shocked to see me. Not delighted or amazed. Shocked. Emily, the other international volunteer, was even more surprised to see me. Roney, a Ugandan volunteer, was the only one who actually seemed happy at my arrival.

I had thought my surprise visit would be seen as exciting and romantic but, seeing the look on Luke's face, I suddenly felt like a creepy stalker. The *buda-buda* man had already taken off and I felt stranded. I had travelled for over three hours to get here and now, in an instant, I wished I could disappear.

Once Luke accepted the fact that I was here, he was polite but in a way that was detached and distant. How could it be that only a week earlier he had come to see me and we had been so close? I felt like an idiot. I stood outside his house, quiet and awkward. Emily offered to show me around. Their house was simple but had large windows so the rooms were a lot lighter than in our place. In Luke's room, my eyes were immediately drawn to the photos that he had stuck on the wall. They were all of his girlfriend, Sarah. I felt completely humiliated but tried to act cool, as if it was fine for him to be treating me like rubbish. As if I didn't care that all the affection he had shown for me had been an act.

The day passed slowly and, as the hours went on, Luke felt more and more like a stranger. When night came, and he and I were sitting in his room, I couldn't help but ask him what was going on—the sudden shift in his behaviour was confusing the hell out of me. He pulled a strange expression, as if he was trying to look sad, but it was obvious he was enjoying himself. He told me that he liked me, but not enough to justify breaking up with Sarah. I said I understood. I didn't want to embarrass myself further by letting on how much I was hurting.

I remembered that I had brought chocolate. I had grabbed it from the supermarket in Kamuli on the way, just as Luke had done when he had visited me. I pulled it out of my bag in an attempt to show there were no hard feelings. That's what I tried to tell myself anyway. In reality I wanted to draw him back to the passionate moment that we had shared a week earlier.

Luke's face lit up when he saw the chocolate . . . And then there was that damn smile again. He really had the biggest smile I had ever seen, it looked like it might stretch right off his cheeks.

Roney and Emily were asleep in another room. In Luke's room it was dark, the only light coming from a lantern in the corner of the room. We were sitting on the mattress. I opened the chocolate and handed it to Luke. He broke some off and then handed it back, our fingers touching as I took it from him. *Oh god.* I was so attracted to him. We both sat quietly, eating our chocolate. And then we kissed.

I truly wanted to believe that whatever I was feeling, Luke felt too. But when the kissing stopped, and Luke fell asleep, I lay awake. I was wondering how I could be aware that I was being a complete idiot and yet still continue to act in such a way. At some point I must have fallen asleep. When I woke at first light, everyone else was still asleep so I tiptoed outside. Unlike our house, where we had neighbours everywhere, their house had plenty of space around it and so I could sit outside in peace.

I thought about my relationship with Luke—how cold and distant he had been when I arrived the day before, and how his behaviour hadn't really changed that much until he kissed me. This was the first time he had acted not just disinterested but unfriendly towards me. Then I remembered when the first time he caught my attention, he was sniggering at a comment that one of the Ugandan volunteers had made. I remembered his reaction to the girl who had stolen his wallet, and how furious and vile he was to the woman in the phone shop. Luke had never hidden this side of him, but before yesterday he had never treated me badly. I was angry with myself that I had been so naïve as to think that I was special, that I was different. But mainly I was disappointed in myself, that I had still been so interested in Luke even after seeing how poorly he treated others. He was self-absorbed and rude and I had realised that, and I had liked him anyway. *Who did that make me?*

It seemed forever until Luke woke up. He woke up as Luke the Jerk, not Nice Luke. He told me how the kissing had been a mistake and that he just wanted to be friends. I agreed that that was best and then had him point me in the direction of the *matatu*. I was ready to go home.

●

I arrived back in Namwendwa before Jane, and of course Lillian and Wemusa were not around. I sat on one of our wooden chairs out the front of the house. I was feeling pretty flat, but I thought that watching the children play would cheer me up. Dawoodee was dribbling with his ball. It seemed like he was constantly practising. His woven ball was beautiful, and I wondered if he had made it himself. I stood up, and gestured for him to come over. He ran over with his ball and we kicked it back and forth. Dawoodee was always barefoot and so I took my sandals off too. I liked the feel of the dirt under my feet.

Suddenly a howling cry came from across the road. It was Kisashi. Her mother was whipping her with a stick. I could hear every blow and could see the raw red marks that it was leaving on the girl's skin. I didn't know what Kisashi had supposedly done wrong, but I did know that physical punishment was common here.

Kisashi looked up—she could see me watching her. I didn't know what to do. My own morals told me that violence was wrong, but who was I to judge that my morals were right? I didn't want to simply assume that I knew best and impose my beliefs on others, because that in itself also seemed immoral. However, recognising the importance of respecting other cultures' ways of doing things was easy in theory, but difficult in practice when just metres away there was a child screaming in pain.

The woman was Dawoodee's mother too. He kicked the ball back to me, encouraging me to keep playing. I returned him the ball and momentarily turned away from Kisashi. But the girl's cries were echoing inside me. Finally I could not stand it any longer and, saying goodbye to Dawoodee, I raced back into our house. I went straight to Jane's and my room. Lying on my bed, I reached for my iPod, put my earphones in and turned it up loud.

Tears came flooding out of me. I was crying for Kisashi. I was crying because I was angry at myself for how I had treated Jack and how I had been such an idiot with Luke. I was crying because I felt totally alone. I turned on my side to face the cement wall. On it I had stuck photos of my younger brother, Josh, which I brought with me from Australia. In one of the photos he was playing the guitar and he had the most joyful smile. Josh loved music and when he played an instrument, or listened to music or danced to it, his whole body would come alive and he was so happy. I reached out to the photo, placing my finger on Josh's face. I wished he were here to give me a hug.

As I was looking at the photo, I realised that, just as the students had done the previous week, when I had been thinking of love I had only considered romantic love. But there were so many special people in my life. In the letter Mum had given me to read on the plane, she had written that when I was born she had been worried that she would not love me enough, as she already loved my brother Sam so much. But once I was born, she realised love was boundless. I was only just starting to understand what she meant by those words. I realised that I was upset because I cared about people. I cared about Kisashi, about Jack and—whether I liked it or not—I cared about Luke. I wasn't alone at all.

Jane bought disinfectant from Jinja and she saturated the bathing area with it. We asked Andrew if he could ask people not to urinate there and he said he would try. The next week we organised a community meeting. It was open for anyone to attend but we specifically invited 30 key players from Namwendwa, such as local council members. The purpose of the meeting was to explain how we were working in the area as health educators, mainly by teaching health in the primary and secondary schools. We also wanted to learn the community's core concerns for Namwendwa.

We were holding the meeting in the local council building. It was a cement block, with open windows and an open space for the door. Inside were wooden benches, and a wooden table and individual chairs up the front for Lillian, Wemusa, Jane, Andrew Opio and myself. The day was scheduled to start at 11 a.m. but by 12.30 p.m. there were still only 12 people present. While we were waiting in hope for others to come, Andrew explained that some people would have liked to attend, but to do so would have meant less time working on their land. The majority of people in Namwendwa lived off sustenance farming, meaning what they grew was what they ate. If they didn't work on the land during the day, then they would literally go hungry that night and so would their family.

Given what Andrew had told us, 12 people suddenly seemed like a reasonable number and we began the meeting. Lillian and Andrew mainly conducted proceedings because it was all in Lusoga, so when one of them wasn't speaking, they were translating for Wemusa, Jane or myself. It was a little frustrating to feel like I was observing the meeting rather than participating in it. No concerns or issues were raised; people mainly just expressed their gratitude for us coming to work in Namwendwa. But I kept thinking about Andrew's comment—the thought of people not being able to leave their land for even a day.

It was a Wednesday and we had no classes in the morning, so Jane and I decided to visit Florence. On the walk to her house my right foot was really bothering me. I seemed to have developed some really large blisters, which was uncommon for me. I assumed it was because I wore the same sandals everywhere and walked so much. I ignored the pain.

When we arrived at the school, a bamboo structure, Florence was teaching the kids a song and we didn't want to interrupt. It was the first time that I had seen a teacher in Namwendwa use creative techniques. Florence was very passionate about her work and her enthusiasm was contagious. As soon as she spotted us by the doorway, she invited us inside. The kids were tiny and adorable—she got them to sing a song for us, and they all clapped in time as well. It was a really happy and positive environment.

We sat in on the class for a while, enjoying watching Florence teach. But we feared our presence was a distraction for the kids, so we decided to leave. When we said goodbye, all the kids clapped and sang in unison, 'Thanks a lot, thanks a lot, and we do it like that every day.' It didn't really make sense; but they had obviously been practising, so we also clapped for them, and then thanked them.

We walked back to our house, picked up our things for teaching and were about to head to the primary school for lunch. Lillian was coming with us. But, as soon as we started walking again, my foot once more felt really sore. I had never realised blisters could be this bad and I mentioned this to the girls. They asked to see. We stopped walking. I took off my right sandal and lifted my foot up.

'Oh, no!' they both exclaimed. 'They're not blisters—you've got jiggers.'

I had never heard of jiggers before but, from the tone of Lillian's and Jane's voices, I figured it wasn't good. Unfortunately I was right. Jiggers meant worms—I had worms living in my foot. Apparently I had got them out of the dirt.

Moments later I was sitting out the front of our house. Jane was sitting in front of me and my foot was resting on her lap. She had spent some time in Costa Rica and had got jiggers there, so she knew all about it and promised to remove the worms painlessly. Everyone came over to watch and offer to help. It was a little nerve-wracking having so many people staring and pointing at my foot. Jane first used a sterilised needle from my medical kit to make a hole in my foot. It didn't hurt because all the skin around the jigger area was dried. She then literally fished out a worm, carefully ensuring that she got all the eggs as well.

Everyone was gasping; they hadn't seen a worm so big. Most people normally recognised straightaway when they had jiggers and removed them when the worms were still small and before there were eggs. Of course I had never even considered that the bump on the sole of my foot was a worm laying eggs.

It took about an hour to remove all the worms and eggs. The worms were thin and long and looked like noodles. After the removal procedure was complete I had an impressive hole in my foot, which Jane covered with a bandage to stop it getting infected. My foot still felt a little funny to walk on, but it was a lot better than it had been.

At last we continued on our way to the primary school. When we got there, most of the teachers were having lunch—*porcho* and beans—but Sam and Andrew were not to be seen. Lillian sat down to eat, while Jane and I asked after Sam and Andrew. One of the teachers, Moses, stood up and had us follow him to a room at the end of one of the classroom blocks.

We found Sam and Andrew in a small room we hadn't seen before; apparently it was the storage room. It was a mess. Sacks of maize, bags of charcoal, rat poo everywhere, but also books. Books! Apparently the government had sent them to the school, but the school didn't really know the best way to store them and now most of them had been chewed apart by rats.

With the discovery of the room and the few uneaten books, Jane and I both had the same thought—the room could be transformed into a library. We asked the men what they thought of this idea and they were very excited. Most of what was in the room was either rubbish or could work as part of the library; as for the sacks of charcoal and maize, Andrew offered to store them in his house.

Moses was especially excited by the library idea, and was literally jumping up and down and clapping his hands. He offered to help us clean up the room. We still had time before we needed to teach; after my foot worm episode I had lost my appetite, so we skipped lunch and set to work.

First we pulled everything out. There were many spider webs with large spiders living in them. But I have never been afraid of spiders—despite knowing the deadliness of their bite, they still look like funny little creatures to me. Harmless rats, on the other hand, I was not a fan of and there were many of them scampering about.

By the time we had cleared the room, it was time for us to teach. Our lesson went well, and Jane and I were in great spirits on the walk back home. We were excited about the library and talking about how we were going to develop it when suddenly I felt an agonising pain on the lower half of my left leg. I looked down, and there was a black bug biting through my skin and burying under it. Instinctively I tried to pull the bug off, but it was stuck. Then I thought I had got it off. But when I looked for it on the ground, it was nowhere to be seen.

8
My Brother Josh

NAMWENDWA, UGANDA, June 2005

The next day I woke to find my leg had inflated like a large sausage balloon. It looked pretty disgusting, but also kind of hilarious. I considered ignoring it but, given we had no lessons organised for the day, Jane convinced me to get it checked out.

There was a medical clinic in Namwendwa but it was understaffed and under-resourced. If we went there, I would probably wait all day and not be seen. So we decided that heading to the clinic in Kamuli was our best bet. As I grabbed my wallet, I was also sure to grab my copy of Lonely Planet's *Healthy Travel Guide—Africa*. Nothing *like a little light reading and self-diagnosis for the bus ride in*, I thought.

At Namwendwa trading centre, the trusted white *matatu*, which had 'God is Great' spray-painted above the front window, was already waiting. Jane and I clambered inside and made our way to the back. There were only three other passengers currently on board—an old man who sat right at the front, and a young woman with her baby. She was sitting in the row in front of us dressed in the traditional *gomesi* and was peering out the window. Her baby was wrapped in a length of material and was tied to her back. Ugandan women always carried their babies on their backs, and they left them tied like this when sitting. This made sense on the woven mats that had no back rests, but on the *matatu* it seemed odd. At first, I felt sorry for the baby in front of me, whose body was pressed against the seat, his little head resting just over it. But he smiled happily. He wasn't even bothered by Jane's and my whiteness, which was a pleasant surprise.

We had to wait for over an hour for the *matatu* to be sufficiently overflowing with passengers, animals and luggage. While we were waiting, I continued to give big grins to the baby in front and, when I was confident that he wasn't about to start howling in fear, I even pulled some silly faces. This was a lot more fun than reading about the potential illnesses I might have had.

When the bus finally rattled on its way, I couldn't help but stare at the baby's bobbing head. It really looked like it might detach from his little body and go flying off at any moment. And yet he was still smiling. *Amazing*. It made me think that we must be far too over-protective of babies back in Australia—they are obviously much tougher than we give them credit for.

Once in Kamuli, Jane and I headed straight to the medical clinic. As we were walking, Jane switched on her phone and almost immediately it started ringing. She answered it and was grinning as she talked. I tried to play detective and work out who the mystery caller was. I assumed it was another SPW volunteer because Jane talked as if the caller knew both this area and me. I guessed it was Lindy as she had been Jane's closest friend during our training.

Suddenly my detective work was interrupted as Jane asked if I wanted to go to Jinja for the day and go to the clinic there instead. Lindy and a few of the other volunteers didn't have to teach this afternoon or Friday so they had headed to Jinja and wanted Jane and me to come too. *So it WAS Lindy calling,* I mused to myself.

I said I was happy to go although it would have to be just a day trip because, unlike the other volunteers, we did have to teach tomorrow. It also meant that we would spend half the day on buses, but Jane and I were so excited by the spontaneity of our decision that we weren't really thinking about the logistics.

We turned back toward the *matatu* station, skipped along the dirt road and then stepped back onto another bus. There were no bobbing-headed babies this time, but a young Ugandan man did declare his love for me and ask whether I was married. I told him that I had a handsome husband and seven children. If I was going to lie, I figured that I might as well make it an interesting one. He laughed at my response, and then asked if I would marry him. Now it was my turn to laugh.

It took half an hour for the bus to fill and then just under two hours to drive to Jinja. Once we arrived, I was keen to get my leg checked out straightaway. Neither Jane nor I had any clue where the medical clinic was, but *buda-buda* men were calling out to us from all directions: 'You come and I take you.' It really did make life easy when you could travel around on the back of a bike.

Jane didn't like the motorbikes; she said they were dangerous, which was true. I liked to think I was young, wild, free and totally invincible, so I thrived on going as fast as possible and didn't particularly like wearing helmets. But I did like being diplomatic, so we agreed for two men on push bikes to take us to the clinic. Admittedly, it was quite peaceful sitting on the back of the push bike but I felt terrible for the man having to pedal along, with his weight and mine.

The Jinja Medical Clinic was a simple building. The reception area consisted of a small room with a woman sitting behind a tiny wooden table, and three wooden chairs for waiting patients. Only the middle chair was occupied, by an elderly woman wearing a lime-green *gomesi*. She had a large lump protruding from the side of her neck. The thing was bigger than a golf ball and looked seriously uncomfortable. I had to keep reminding myself to stop staring.

Jane and I approached the woman behind the desk and I asked her if I could see a doctor. The woman gave me a blank expression so I took a step back and pointed to my enlarged leg. The woman peered over her desk, glanced briefly at my badly swollen limb, and then pointed to the chairs.

Jane and I took a seat either side of the woman with the lump on her neck. As the three of us sat silently, I thought how bizarre it was that we were the only patients waiting. It's like when you go out to a restaurant—you don't want to go somewhere that is so busy that you can't hear yourself think, but you also don't want to go somewhere that is dead, because what does that say about the food . . .

As I began to wonder what other clinics there might be in Jinja, a man in a white coat appeared. He was Ugandan and quite young for a doctor, early thirties maybe. He gestured for Jane and me to follow him out of the reception and into his office next door. We left the other woman still waiting. *She really should have been called first*, I thought. I hated white privilege.

The doctor's office was as basic as the reception room, consisting only of yet another wooden table and a few chairs. He asked Jane and me to sit and then asked what was wrong. I showed him my leg and explained about the bug. The young doctor made a loud 'hmmm' sound, as though he was going to say something profound. But instead he shook his head and said he didn't know what the bug was or why my leg was inflated.

I sat dumbfounded. *Is this really a medical clinic? And is this really a doctor?* I wasn't convinced.

Jane pulled out my African health book and began flipping through the pages about insect bites, reading aloud the names of the different creatures, as if it might spur an epiphany from this supposed doctor. But the man just continued to shake his head.

After Jane had read out almost every possibility from my health book, she insisted the doctor at least do some blood tests. He moaned, but then agreed. He popped out of the room, returning a few moments later with needles in his hand. I looked in the other direction as he stepped toward my arm. And then in went the needle. *Ouch*. But suddenly the needle was out. I sighed in relief and then ... jab, the needle went in again. *What?*

I turned my head to face this man and asked him what he was doing. He told me that my veins were too small and hard to find, and then he stabbed me for the third time. *Definitely not a doctor*, I concluded.

Fortunately, with the third jab, he was able to draw blood successfully. But then he announced that the results would not be ready until the next day. *So much for getting back to Namwendwa ...* So Jane and I made the impulsive decision to spend the night in Jinja. We didn't really have a choice. In the morning we would get my results, and then hopefully we would get back to the village in time to teach in the afternoon.

As we left the clinic, I couldn't work out what was worse—my magnified leg or my weak skewered arm. But whatever, I followed Jane to the backpackers hostel, which was conveniently only a ten-minute walk away.

As Jane checked us in, I raced straight to the toilet. It was a normal flushing toilet but it now felt a little strange to simply sit down, as opposed to squatting. As nice as it was not to be surrounded by flies, cockroaches or snakes, when

I flushed the toilet it felt like an immense waste of water. *That would be two trips to the borehole*, I thought to myself.

As I was washing my hands, I looked up and was confronted with myself—literally. I didn't have a mirror in the village and so this was the first time I had seen my reflection in months. My face was rounder. I sighed—Sam's prediction was proving true and I was putting on weight. I wasn't quite at the sumo wrestler stage yet, but I certainly wasn't thin anymore either. It was seriously annoying to be gaining weight from food I didn't even enjoy—it was all so heavy and bland. If I was going to become fat, I felt it should have been from chocolate and ice cream, not *porcho* and rice and *matooke*. *Gah.*

I forced myself to stop the internal whining and went to find Jane. I popped my head into a dorm room, but she wasn't there. Then I heard voices from the main room.

The backpackers was a pretty cool spot to hang out; in the main room it had a bar, pool table, stereo and couches. I wandered in and found not only Jane and Lindy but also many of the other volunteers, Luke included. *Shit*, I thought. *So this is how our paths cross next—when my leg looks like a tree stump and I've just realised that I'm a fatty. Deep breaths, act cool*, I told myself and tried to ignore him. He was also apparently ignoring me. I wondered what Lindy and the others must have been thinking. The last time we had all been together, Luke and I had been best friends, but now we were acting like strangers.

I was making a considerable effort to seem happy when talking to the other girls and I was making a joke of my mega leg, when a good-looking guy asked if I wanted to play pool with him. I was pleasantly surprised that anyone would even talk to me while I looked so repulsive, and said that I would love to play.

As it turned out, he was very friendly, a volunteer on another program. As we chatted and played pool, I couldn't help but sneak glances at Luke. He looked as uncomfortable as I had felt moments earlier. *He's jealous*, I smiled to myself.

That night in bed, it dawned on me that everything with Luke had forced me to seriously analyse my relationship with Jack. I had realised that I had really only been with Jack because I felt a need to be in a relationship. Now it seemed obvious that I hadn't changed when I came to Uganda—I simply shifted from Jack fulfilling that need to Luke.

Luke had ultimately rejected me, but tonight made me understand that I could find someone else to fill that need if I wanted to. However, finally realising that I did actually have a choice about whether I was in a relationship, suddenly made me feel very happy to be on my own. That was what I actually wanted, and it's what I had wanted all along—I just had to know that I had a choice.

In the morning, Jane and I returned to the medical clinic. The blood tests had not shown anything and so the doctor decided to start me on antibiotics. He also gave me an injection in my hand, who knows what for.

Before returning to Namwendwa, we went to a shop connected to the internet. I emailed various people to canvass the possibility of the Heart Foundation donating some skipping ropes for the schools in Namwendwa. Jane wrote to her family and friends to see if anyone would donate some money for us to buy new books for the library that we were setting up in the primary school.

Next we popped into the SPW office to see if we had received any post. Irene and I were both on our best behaviour and made polite small talk. I was excited to have a parcel from Mum. I also had eight letters from Jack. He had written all of them before we had broken up and they were all so loving and kind, but I felt detached reading his words. There was no doubt in my mind that I had made the right decision in ending things, but I knew I had treated Jack terribly. It would take me a long time to forgive myself for that.

●

My leg soon deflated back to a normal size and life in the village was going well. We bought tins of paint and brushes from one of the little hardware shops in Kamuli, and completed the first coat of white for the inside of the library. Nowhere else in Namwendwa was painted. Houses and buildings were either mud-brick or grey from being plastered. Making things look aesthetically pleasing wasn't exactly a priority for people in the community, so at first I wondered whether it was a poor use of funds to paint the inside of the room. But when I talked to Andrew and Moses about it, they thought that painting was a simple way to make the room special. As we were painting, I realised how true this was.

The teachers really enjoyed helping to paint. It was a new experience for them, and it was magical to see the room being transformed with every brush stroke. I noticed how, if people had a question or comment, these were always directed to Jane rather than me. I told myself that it was because she was older, but it was still irritating. Moses continued to be particularly enthusiastic about the project, and was so kind and helpful. When we completed the first coat of paint, which didn't take long, he smiled and said, 'Many hands make light work.'

I loved this philosophy of working together and the cooperative spirit it inspired. I really noticed how the sense of community was valued here. It made me think about how, back in Australia, I had often heard it said that poor people seem to be happy. It felt like this comment was made as a justification for allowing people to continue to be disadvantaged, rather than empowering them.

The problem with saying that poor people seem happy is that it implies that people are happy because they are poor, which is a little ridiculous, I thought. It would be a mistake to think that people who are poor are not aware of their situation and would not wish for better. Which is obvious really—who would be happy to be in a situation where they cannot afford treatment when their child is sick? And yet, people did seem happier here. It appeared to me that the difference with people here, as opposed to people I knew in Australia, was their values. People here valued their health, their family, their friendships, their community and God. My own values in Australia hadn't included any of these things. My checklist for happiness had revolved around good grades, having a cute boyfriend, being fit and skinny. It felt like these were the things that were generally valued in our society. Even the cartoon movies that I had watched as a child involved the vulnerable girl going from rags to riches, while being swept off her feet by the handsome prince.

When I was in Year 12, I was achieving all the things that society applauds—I was School Captain, I was academically soaring, I had a boyfriend who hid flowers in my school locker, I had a reasonable part-time job... life should have been perfect. But instead I was the saddest and most confused that I had ever been. My instinct was nagging at me, at first whispering and then shouting. It told me that there were no clear-cut criteria for happiness. And what I perceived society to consider the *good life* might not in fact be the good life for me. At school, I was happiest when I was helping other people, my community.

That was the truth, and perhaps an important explanation for how I had ended up in Uganda. For me the fairytale was in losing the prince, standing strong on my own two feet and living simply. My life here in Uganda was based purely on the values of family, friendship and community. And right now, in this moment, I was the happiest I had ever been.

It was strange how I had become so used to life in Namwendwa that I almost stopped noticing things that a few months earlier would have been obvious. This happened to me one afternoon when teaching basic sanitation in the primary school. I had been talking about the importance of washing your hands after going to the latrine, when one of the students raised his hand and pointed out that they had nowhere to wash their hands at the primary school. I felt awful and embarrassed when I realised he was right. There was no running water in Namwendwa and the nearest borehole to the primary school was kilometres away. While water was collected for cooking and drinking, it was not made accessible to the students.

The latrines the students used were extremely dirty, probably in a worse state than the community latrine near my house. Add to this that everyone in the community ate with their hands, so having clean hands was essential—and yet was not even a possibility for the kids with the current set-up.

Jane and I spoke to Andrew and Moses about this and together we planned how we could create some basic hand-washing facilities. The four of us went to Kamuli, where we were able to buy large green tins and some taps. A local labourer was able to attach the taps to the tins for us. Andrew and Moses then used sticks to construct stands for the tins. It was an extremely simple design—each tin's lid could easily be lifted so the tin could be filled with water every morning. Then the kids could just turn on the tap. Andrew and Moses even drew up a roster so that different kids would collect the water each day.

When I saw the students washing their hands, it was amazing. Something so simple might prevent the kids from getting sick. It was also an incredible feeling—the kids themselves had identified that having nowhere to wash their hands was a problem and then, after brainstorming and working with the community, we had created an effective and sustainable solution. This was development at its best.

●

Wemusa had been strangely nice lately. He had even cooked us dinner a few times. It was still just rice, but he made it at 6 p.m. rather than at 10 p.m. and he actually made enough for all of us. By Wemusa's standards, this was a pretty big effort.

He had also been showing appreciation when we did things for him. It was so nice to feel the tension within the house disappearing and a bond forming between us. I had seen a glimpse of this side of him when he played the warrior and killed the rat, but now he seemed to be that cheerful guy all the time. I had no idea what had brought about this sudden change, but it was bliss. Now the only thing missing was Lillian.

In fact, every day just kept getting better. One day Jane and I were walking to the trading centre when we stopped under the shade of a giant tree to have a drink. While we were standing on the side of the dusty red road, behind us an aged man sat outside his house watching us. Finally, he gestured for us to come and join him.

He was a tiny man; his skin clung to the bones of his aged body and the few teeth he had were rotten yellow. Yet he had the most friendly and welcoming smile we had ever seen. He happily chatted to us in Lusoga and we made *hmmm* and *ahhhhh* sounds when we thought it appropriate. Finally he said a word we understood—*avocado*. Our grins widened and, almost in unison, we replied, '*Nyenda avocadoes.*' (We like avocadoes.)

The rainy season had just started and so we had enjoyed a few avocadoes up to now. But before we knew what was happening, the fragile man was hobbling back into his house. His home, like most around here, was a small mud hut with open spaces for a door and windows. Jane and I looked at each other awkwardly for a moment, wondering whether we should continue on our way, when the man suddenly re-appeared. He was cradling six large perfect avocadoes.

Jane and I stared in amazement as he placed three of them in Jane's hands and three in mine. We thanked him repeatedly and he flashed us his golden smile. It was an incredible gesture, and the sort of kindness I would remember for life. He had basically just given us, complete strangers, everything he had.

Now that I felt like I had truly found my place within the village, I no longer thought it was necessary to do things I didn't actually believe in. In other words, I stopped going to church. Namwendwa felt deserted on Sunday mornings; Jane and I were possibly the only people not worshipping. On this particular Sunday morning we had just finished having some porridge. It was beautiful and peaceful outside and Jane was sitting on the woven mat, while I was standing closer to our house washing the morning dishes. Jane seemed strangely quiet, fixated on something. I followed her stare—across the road, lying in the dirt was a child.

I knew straightaway that this child had an intellectual disability and probably some physical disabilities too. It pained me to watch her. Not because she couldn't walk or because she was lying there helplessly. It pained me because I had been living here for months now and this was the first time I had seen her. Every night I played with her siblings—Victoria, Mirimu, Kisashi and Dawoodee. I had spoken to her father several times about his children, but never had this child received a mention. I realised immediately that this child was not to be spoken about and not to be seen. I knew that she would be considered a shame on the family and therefore she was to be hidden away. Today, however, her family was at church and she had used her elbows to drag herself outside.

I raced inside and grabbed some toy cars that Jane and I sometimes used when playing with the other kids. Then Jane and I approached the girl; we sat on the dirt about 3 metres away from her. A rag-like dress hung off her dirt-covered body. She wore no underpants and the distinctive smell of urine filled the air. I was surprised to see that her breasts were large, because the rest of her body looked under-developed. She was not a child, but a young woman. She lay with her face toward the ground. Her body was unnaturally twisted and her feet, in particular, appeared small and deformed.

Jane and I greeted her in Lusoga, but she did not look up. When a child raced past, skipping on her way home from church, we asked her if she knew the name of the young woman in front of us. The child paused for a moment, and then told us that the woman's name was Kigali. The child then continued on her way.

Jane and I added the name Kigali to our greeting and eventually the young woman looked up. As she did so, I was startled to see that she was clenching a stick in her mouth and it was dripping with saliva. I took a deep breath and then started playing with the little cars, pushing them back and forth, making the relevant car sounds. The stick fell to the ground as Kigali laughed. Her smile was big and beautiful.

Jane and I moved a little closer and together we sang, '*If you are happy and you know it, clap your hands . . .*' Once more, Kigali laughed.

More people were now returning from church, so Jane and I retreated to our house. We watched helplessly as people walked past Kigali. Most ignored her, but some kicked her or spat on her—it was horrifying. I allowed myself to cry. At first it was just a few tears and I wiped them away with my arm. But then the tears came flooding and I raced to my bed. I had been on such a high recently, viewing everything positively, but I couldn't do that now.

I lay on my bed, my body curled up, facing the cement wall. Again, I found myself face-to-face with the photograph of Josh. My little brother who could light up my world with just a smile. My little brother who gave the warmest hugs imaginable. My little brother with Down syndrome.

In that moment my two worlds—my Australian life and my Ugandan life—came crashing together. I buried my face in my hands. Every part of me was aching; my mind was a collision of thoughts. *Fuck.* I didn't know how to cope with this intensity of emotions. I looked at the photo of Josh again and wondered if it could really be a coincidence that my house was opposite Kigali's and that our paths had now crossed. While I was thinking of Josh, and missing him, in my heart I also made a promise to Kigali—*I will remember you*.

I was restless trying to sleep that night and my dreams were strange. I dreamt of my dog, Chicago. She was a beautiful dog with energy and cheekiness in excess. But in my dream she was weak. Not at all like the Chicago I knew and loved. I woke at 1 a.m. and couldn't get back to sleep. *Something's wrong*, I just knew it. By 9 a.m. I couldn't stand the anxiety any longer, and I walked to the trading centre. During May the promised telephone tower had been built near Florence's home and school so now I had phone reception. I desperately wanted to speak to Mum.

I dialled her number. It was only the second time that I'd called her since being away, the other time being after I had ended things with Jack. She picked up straightaway and, from the slight tremble in her voice, I knew immediately that something really was wrong. She told me that after I left Australia Chicago had become increasingly ill. She had developed a tumour and ultimately lost all her senses. Mum told me how awful it had been to watch Chicago bumping into things and falling over. Yesterday afternoon she had been put down. Just like that, my beautiful dog was gone. I was grateful that I hadn't seen her deteriorate, and that I had only happy memories. But I also wanted to find a way to say goodbye.

I returned to my Namwendwa home and sat on my bed and cried. Once I had calmed down, I wrote a eulogy for 'the crazy black beast', as Dad had often referred to her. It seemed like the only way to deal with my feelings was by putting them on paper. I didn't know if Chicago visiting me in my dreams meant anything of significance, and I didn't really care. I just hoped she would visit me again.

The next day Jane and I went to the health clinic in Namwendwa to ask the doctor-in-charge some questions about disabilities. The health clinic was located along the road between Kamuli and Namwendwa trading centre. It was a government health clinic for four villages and was terribly under-resourced. There was one doctor and four nurses for a population of over 55 000 people. Not surprisingly, there was never enough time for people to be informed, consulted or treated properly. If someone showed any symptoms of malaria, which could be anything from a fever to a headache, then they would be given treatment without even having a blood test to confirm they actually did have malaria. Treatment was given out so frequently that many people in the village suspected that the mosquitoes were now actually becoming resistant to the treatment. It was all pretty scary and concerning, but this was not the reason for our visit.

We had a million questions for the doctor, but seeing the never-ending line of patients waiting outside, we tried to prioritise our queries. We wanted to know whether babies were diagnosed with a disability at birth; if so, was a record kept? What knowledge was there in Namwendwa about different types of disabilities, and was there any support for people with disabilities and their families?

The doctor was helpful but understandably rushed in responding to each question. We learnt that a baby might be diagnosed with a disability at birth, but normally only if it was a visible physical disability. Sometimes a record was kept of this, but he wasn't sure where. There was a little bit of knowledge about physical disabilities in the area. If someone could not walk, or had some other obvious physical disability, then they were called lame. There was no knowledge at all about intellectual disabilities. Most people in the community believed that to have a child with a disability was to be cursed by God. And there were no forms of support for people with disabilities.

We left the clinic disheartened. I wondered how many kids were hidden away in houses. I thought that there was a clear difference between simply imposing my morals on others and offering more information about such matters.

Back at our home, I grabbed the photo of Josh from my wall and took it to Kigali's house across the road. Her father, Paddy, was out the front. I greeted him, and then I showed him the photograph of Josh. I told Paddy all about Josh—not just about his disability, but everything he was capable of, and how special he was to me. Paddy was surprised by what I said. I got the impression that he hadn't realised that there were people with disabilities in the Western world too, and that we didn't consider such disabilities to be God's curse. He really listened to what I said. I didn't mention Kigali. I didn't need to.

The second coat of white paint for the inside of the primary school library had now been completed. The bookcases had also been constructed. We had employed a local labourer to make two of them out of local timber and they looked amazing. He'd even varnished them. It cost $100 for the wood and the labour involved. Jane and I covered it but we told the school that the money was from SPW and told SPW that the school paid for it.

Even with just the paint and the bookcases, the room looked unbelievable. Jane and I were hopeful that we would be able to fill the new shelves with books, and we also planned to make wall displays. I was so excited. This was definitely my favourite project.

But even this delight and the joys of the rainy season—mangoes and avocadoes—were no longer enough to keep me smiling. It was mesmerising to sit inside the house and watch the rain pounding down outside, but it was terribly inconvenient when you actually wanted to do something. It continued to be warm, but it could literally rain all day. It was basically impossible to teach. At the primary school, the rain would flood in. The dirt ground on which the kids sat would turn to mud, and it was impossible to hear each other because the hammering of the drops hitting the tin roof was deafening. Kids would just run home.

It was hard to go about daily tasks as well. We normally cooked outside because the house had little ventilation, but with the rain we were now forced to use the charcoal stove inside and the house quickly filled with smoke. It was hard to see with all the smoke. Sometimes it was hard to breathe too.

Going to the latrine was also difficult. You would have to tread slowly to get there because of the slippery mud and so, each time you went, you got saturated. But the thing that bothered me the most were the toads. They were everywhere! Giant, slimy toads. Sometimes the floor in our house was almost covered with them, and we had to keep sweeping them out! At least the rats would run away, but the toads just sat there and you constantly had to watch your step. *Yuk!*

⬤

It was Wemusa's birthday. Birthdays were not normally celebrated here, but Jane and I wanted to do something special for him. Wemusa absolutely loved music and we had bought him a Walkman from Kamuli. Our friends in the supermarket had even wrapped it for us.

When Wemusa left for the latrine this particular morning, Jane and I grabbed his present and carefully placed it on one of the wooden chairs in the main room. Then we moved the chair so that it was blocking the entrance to his room. When he returned from the latrine, his eyes widened with disbelief and excitement. He was frozen still, staring at the wrapped box.

Eventually Jane and I grew impatient. We made it clear that the gift was for him and encouraged him to open it. When he finally tore open the floral paper, his reaction could not have been better. He was so happy. It was the sort of happiness that shows in every part of your face and body—he was beaming.

During the day, Lillian returned from her latest disappearance and so we had a full house. We planned to take Wemusa out to dinner at the trading centre but when it came time to leave, he couldn't be found. Lillian said that she thought he was planning to meet us there, so we started the walk.

Of course it rained and by the time we reached the trading centre, 2 kilometres away, we were drenched. Lillian wore a plastic bag on her head to protect her hair. She really made me laugh. It was nice to have her home, even if it was only fleetingly. Once we got to the trading centre, we still couldn't find Wemusa but we were starving, so we decided to eat anyway. Rice and beans was the only thing on offer. God, I missed variety. I was seriously craving vegetables.

Dessert was more exciting. My aunty, Sharon, had sent me a parcel which included a packet of Scotch Finger biscuits. They were absolutely divine—but I didn't want to think about the effect on my waistline. I could almost imagine my whole body expanding with every bite. And yet we still managed to gobble down every biscuit, even licking up the crumbs. They really were irresistible!

When we were finished, there were still no signs of Wemusa and outside it was rainy and dark. The thought of walking home was not at all appealing. So we ended up paying for a *matatu* conductor to drive us home. It felt extremely lavish to have the entire bus to ourselves, when we were normally squashed into some uncomfortable position. But we didn't feel guilty—we enjoyed our lovely ride home.

Back at the house, we were surprised to find Wemusa. He told us that he had had a good night, but he didn't reveal any more details. He was a real dark horse, that boy.

9

How We Cope

NAMWENDWA, UGANDA, July 2005

I was in Jinja, sitting in my favourite internet cafe. I had come here for a day trip to check my emails and check in with SPW. The rain was bucketing down outside and the bus ride had been pretty scratchy. The *matatus* were manic enough when the roads were dry, but muddy roads made for a slippery ride. It didn't really bother me though—I felt stupidly invincible.

While my emails were downloading, I was indulging myself with a cookie. It was a peanut butter and chocolate cookie, and it was divine. I contemplated having a second cookie. When I tilted my head back I could see the jar of them sitting on the counter, luring me. I was about to give in to temptation when I realised my emails had finished downloading.

One of them was from the mum of one of my friends. She worked in the canteen at a primary school in Adelaide and had written with the good news that the Heart Foundation was happy to donate ropes for Namwendwa, and that the school she worked for had held a casual clothes day to raise the money to post the ropes to Uganda. At first I was delighted, but as I read the email again I wanted to bang my head against the computer. I had been a complete idiot. Somehow I had managed to forget the very obvious fact that there would be postage costs; while it was kind of the school to donate this amount, it suddenly made this whole idea seem ridiculous. I could have just purchased the ropes in Kampala, the capital of Uganda, for the same cost as posting the donated ropes. That would have been more time-effective and in a minor way it would have supported the Ugandan economy too. *Gah! Why didn't I think of this earlier?*

I sighed. Really I should have asked the teachers at the schools whether they thought skipping ropes were even a good idea and, if they did, I should have asked their opinion about the best way to source them. They probably would have suggested we just buy ordinary rope from Kamuli and cut it into different sizes as required for the students.

But it was too late now for contemplating what I should have done. The school in Australia had already posted the ropes. I wrote back and thanked my friend's mum. Then I promised myself that the next time I had a grand idea

Me teaching at Namwendwa Primary School—even here the kids were taller than me. My expression gives away how nervous I was. *Photo courtesy of Jane Barett*

The handwashing facilities that we made for the primary school. This came about after I had been teaching hygiene and the kids said they had nowhere to wash their hands. *One Village collection*

Victoria and Sara. They attached groundnuts to their ears to have earrings like mine. Cutest kids ever. *One Village collection*

My friend Dawoodee with younger brother Michael. *One Village collection*

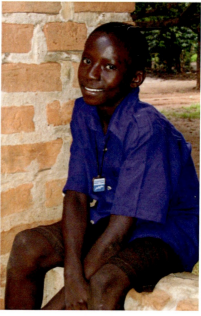

Dawoodee. *One Village collection*

The Community Health Day that we hosted in Namwendwa. *One Village collection*

Family and friendship are one and the same in Namwendwa. *Photo courtesy of Lisa Duffy*

A room we found in Namwendwa Primary School and decided to turn into a library (the room, left side). *One Village collection*

The room, right side. *One Village collection*

In Jane's and my room sewing ribbon borders onto the wall displays that we made for the library. *Photo courtesy of Jane Barett*

Namwendwa Primary School library completed (left side). A little hard work can make a really big difference! *One Village collection*

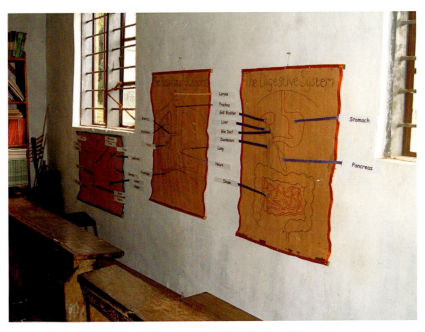

Namwendwa Primary School library completed (right side). From sacks of maize to AMAZING! *One Village collection*

The first eight scholarship girls (2005) in the scheme that Jane and I founded. *One Village collection*

Teaching Andrew how to use a digital camera (2007). *One Village collection*

The Infant School destroyed by termites (2006). A sad day. *One Village collection*

The Infant School new building (2007) and a lot of very happy kids. *One Village collection*

Local boys sit among the maize. In Namwendwa maize is a staple food and is roasted, boiled, used to make porridge and also porcho (or as I prefer to call it, flavourless glug). *One Village collection*

The community celebrates the work of One Village (2007). A beautiful moment. *One Village collection*

about what was in the best interests of someone or a group of people, I would actually ask them first. I also decided this was the first and last time that I would arrange for things to be posted from Australia. I suspected that people would generally prefer donating objects as opposed to cash. However, the reality was that it was more cost-effective, time-effective, sustainable and beneficial for the local economy to buy items in the country for which they were intended.

On my way back from Jinja, the rain finally took a break. I was hoping it would stay away until I got back to Namwendwa—I didn't feel like a mud-sludge-water-ride of a walk home.

By the time we got to Kamuli, the sun had come out. I bumped into Lillian there—she was on her way to her teaching job, but she had some spare time and so she invited me to her family home. I had actually forgotten that Lillian was from Kamuli; it only took a few minutes to walk to her house. I was a little bit taken aback as we entered her home. There were a few bare cement bedrooms around a central open dirt area that Lillian told me was used for cooking, washing and relaxing. With the rain, it had turned into a muddy mess.

Obviously our living conditions in Namwendwa were even worse, but this was different. I knew that Lillian had received a scholarship to go to university; she was a qualified teacher and she had a job. Yet this was her home. It felt like Lillian had done everything in her power to improve the situation for her family, but she still struggled to be able to afford to send her younger siblings to school or get them medication if they were ill. It seemed like Lillian had tried—and was still trying absolutely everything—to support her family, but it wasn't enough. It saddened me to think that realistically there wasn't much else that Lillian could do.

While we were at Lillian's home, she continued to get ready for work. I noticed that she put talcum powder on her face and asked what she was doing. She told me that she wanted lighter skin. I laughed and told her that I wanted a tan.

When I arrived back in Namwendwa the ground had nearly dried and it was getting late. I walked home quickly, keen to get there before it became dark. Jane was outside cooking when I arrived and to the left of our house four women were kneeling in a circle. They wore bangles around their wrists, and around their necks they had each tied a large seed, which had hair dangling from it. One of the women was smoking an old wooden pipe and they all seemed to be both chanting and squabbling at once. Witch doctors! Witch doctors were sitting out the front of our house! I stood near our door, not wanting to be intrusive, but also ensuring I had a clear view.

I asked Jane what was going on but she was as clueless as me. She said the women had been there for over an hour. She had noticed them pushing objects between each other but she hadn't been able to work out what the objects were. I was wide-eyed watching, but Jane suggested that perhaps I shouldn't stare quite so obviously—witch doctors were not the sort of people you wanted to upset.

I leant over the stove and stirred the beans while keeping the women in view. But it seemed I was already too late and had missed the magic, because the women soon stood and wandered down the dirt road. When they had completely disappeared, I charged up to Andrew's shop at the opposite end of the cement block to our house and questioned him about the women. He informed me that they had not actually been performing any magic; rather, they had been distributing the payment from their last job.

It was all very mysterious and intriguing. I asked Andrew what sort of work they did and he informed me that their speciality was removing demons from people's bodies, a pricey exercise. He said they also performed rituals to cure more common illnesses and that this service was more affordable. I wanted to know more. What exactly was pricey? What did these rituals consist of?

Andrew did not know exactly—he did not like to use their services himself. It seemed very strange, but then I suppose that different forms of alternative medicine are used all around the world. However, just as I was pondering this, he went on to tell me that he had heard that some witch doctors sacrificed children to keep the spirits happy. He added that the witch doctors claimed that the spirits demanded both human blood and human organs, especially the heart. *Whoa!* This wasn't just strange anymore, it was seriously concerning. I queried why the police didn't do anything and Andrew told me that the police were scared of the evil spirits too. *Shit.*

Early the next morning there was an intruder in Jane's and my room. I woke to find the mysterious creature attached to the outside of my mozzie net. I looked through my net at the blackish thing above and assumed it was a rat. I snuggled down deeper into the safety of my sleeping bag and hoped it would not poo or urinate on me. I tried to make loud shuffling noises as I restlessly turned backwards and forwards in my sleeping bag, hoping that I might 'accidentally' wake Jane up.

It worked. From her own bed, Jane studied the creature, but she didn't think it was a rat. Then it started moving up the net until it was directly above my head. *Enough!* I carefully lifted the net up and slid out of my bed. The creature stayed attached. *What was that thing?*

Lillian was not around, and I didn't want to wake Wemusa so I scurried next door and found Robert, one of the neighbourhood boys, and asked him if he would help me. Jane, Robert and I were then huddled in the tiny bedroom with Jane and me staying by the door, ready to escape.

Robert opened the small window in our room and then held my net close to it, hoping the creature would want to make its escape. But it remained very still. Robert poked it with his finger. Nothing. He poked again, and then some wings were flung out from what had appeared as just a tight black ball. The mystery creature was a bat! It suddenly flew out the window. I wondered if it had come with the witch doctors. There had been bats in our room many times before, but they normally sat on the high beams that supported the roof. I was happy with them there and even gave them each personal names, but I didn't like them being stuck on my net, just above my head. Damn bats, rats and toads. *Yuk.*

I was singing and dancing out the front of our house, and Victoria was in a fit of giggles watching me. I realise that this is a sweeping generalisation but all Africans (in my vast experience of the continent, *ha ha . . .*) seem to be incredible dancers. The way they move their hips, with their straw skirts reserved especially for dancing, swaying and swishing about, is almost hypnotising. By contrast, I looked like a drunken baboon as I grooved about. But the wonderful thing about dancing is that it is ridiculously infectious fun, no matter how hopeless you are.

The reason for my hilarious boogieing was that we had just received the news that Jane's mum had done a legendary job and raised over $1000. The money was for us to buy books for the primary school library. Jane and I went to the primary school to deliver the good news. The teachers were ecstatic, and we made a list of the textbooks or other books that each of them thought would either assist with their teaching or just be of interest to the kids. While we were chatting it turned out, very conveniently, to be lunchtime and so the cook served us up some *porcho* and beans.

We were chomping away when a tiny boy dressed in his pink school T-shirt and black shorts was flung to the ground nearby. Towering above him was one of the male teachers, and he was shouting at the boy. I couldn't understand what he was saying because it was all in Lusoga. Momentarily he paused and turned to another student who was innocently walking past, directing his yelling towards this boy instead. This time he was shouting an order. The student took off, but soon returned carrying a large stick.

The smaller boy was still in the dirt. He was curled into a small ball and was shaking. The teacher stood above him once more, this time with the stick in his hand. He shouted again and the boy obediently unravelled himself, lying flat out, with his tummy on the ground. The teacher then raised his stick and whipped it hard against the boy's back. He whipped him again, and again, and again. The boy's T-shirt was ripped apart and his back was bleeding in clearly defined lines where the stick had struck. He was wailing in agony.

The other teachers ignored the entire scenario, continuing with their lunch as if this was normal—which, sadly, it was. I closed my eyes and, when I did so, I saw Kisashi who I had seen being beaten by her mother a few months earlier. When the ordeal was over, the boy hobbled away. The teacher sat down and the cook bought him lunch.

I couldn't help myself—I asked what the boy had done wrong. The teacher told me that he had caught the boy stealing groundnuts on the school's land. Basically all food in Namwendwa had to be cooked, so it wasn't like students could just bring a sandwich for lunch. Instead they were expected to bring some maize to contribute and, if they did so, then the school cook would serve them lunch. If not, then they would go hungry. Out of the 1500 plus students at Namwendwa primary, less than 200 were able to bring maize to contribute. The families of the other students did not have any surplus for their children to bring. People in the community also didn't eat breakfast. This meant that the majority of kids were only eating dinner—if that.

No wonder the boy had stolen the groundnuts—he was probably starving. Now he was hungry and beaten. His shirt had also been destroyed and I imagined that he would be dealt another thrashing at home for that. Students weren't meant even to come to school if they didn't have a uniform, and the boy wouldn't have another one. This whipping might have cost him more than his skin and his shirt—he might end up losing his chance of an education.

I hadn't wanted to impose my values—but maybe it was okay to just express my opinion? I looked to Jane, and her face was covered in worry. I knew we were on the same wavelength.

After lunch as we walked home Jane and I decided that the next day we would ask the teachers if they would be interested in a workshop on 'alternative discipline methods'. If they were keen on the idea, then we would find another organisation to come in and run it professionally.

Once we reached home, our conversation switched to discussing the wall displays that we planned to make for the library. Andrew and Moses had found large pieces of bark paper for us to draw on. We planned to draw different parts of the body and label them. We wanted to make the displays interactive as we thought the students would then get more out of them. Ideally we wanted the labels on the wall separate from the drawings, and for the students to be able to move them to their appropriate places on each picture. But we had no idea how we were going to do this.

We could get the labels typed, printed and laminated in Jinja. This was a start. Jane suggested that her parents, who were flying over to visit next month, could bring velcro, which we could use to attach to each label and on the picture. I wasn't keen on this. I had already decided that I didn't think having anything imported (regardless of how convenient it might be) was a good idea. If the velcro fell off the labels or the pictures, it wouldn't be able to be replaced.

Jane thought that if this happened they would then just make do with what they had. On the other hand, I thought we should make do in the first instance. I felt that using things that we could source locally would make the project more sustainable. In all this discussion, I believed we were simply exploring various options for making the wall displays and considering objections to them, but somehow it seemed to be more than that. It turned out that we were having an argument.

Jane went outside, saying she needed some air. I sat inside, not knowing what to do. Jane was my best friend here; we shared *everything* and us getting along was very important to me. But surely we didn't have to see eye-to-eye on everything. Surely it was good to challenge each other.

Jane came back inside and suggested we talk about things. *Did she mean the wall displays or our friendship?* Apparently the latter. She said we spent too much time together. She was right, but being around each other was sort of unavoidable, given our beds were about 30 centimetres apart and we also taught together.

But it wasn't just that. Everyone turned to Jane more than they turned to me, and they frequently compared us: 'Jane speaks so much more Lusoga than you', 'Jane is much thinner than you' and so on. I had become accustomed to Ugandan honesty but it still sometimes ate away at me. I almost feared that, if I were not constantly with Jane, then I would just be left out of things.

It was as though my fate had been sealed from our first week, when we were given village names. Jane was called Babida and I was Kawooda. Whenever twins were born in the village, the oldest was always named Babida and the youngest Kawooda. The community struggled to tell Jane and I apart when we first arrived, both being white and all. What they had known was that Jane was older and so it had stuck that I was 'Little Sister'.

Sometimes it felt like I could have disappeared and no-one would have noticed. I knew that I was as passionate, determined and willing as Jane so it was difficult to be treated differently. Everyone would have felt awful if they understood how painful some of their honest comments were, or how hurtful it was not to feel included. I never voiced these feelings. I didn't want people to feel bad, or for Jane to feel guilty. But I realised that perhaps I was being so strong in my opinion now because I just wanted to be heard. Maybe I was wrong about the velcro, maybe I was being too stubborn. Then again, maybe we should have been having this discussion with Andrew and Moses. In the end I agreed with Jane. Velcro it would be. I was desperate for the tension in the air to dissipate.

•

Jane and I went to Kampala, the big dirty capital, to find the books the teachers had requested and also to meet up with a group that supported people with disabilities. It was good for us to be on a mission, giving us something to talk about and drawing us together again.

We visited all the bookstores first and were happy to be able to get everything on our list. But there were way too many books for us to carry them around with us. Since we had bought the majority of them from one store, they agreed to deliver them to Namwendwa for us. This was a massive weight off our shoulders (literally) and we organised for them to be transported to Namwendwa the following day.

Next Jane and I went to visit a disability support group, where we spoke with a man named Richard. He was physically disabled, missing the lower part of each of his arms, so that his hands were attached at his elbows. He told us his story.

When he was born, the people of his village deemed him useless and wanted to kill him. Even his father agreed that it was the right thing to do. But Richard's mother had taken him in her arms and stated that if they wanted to kill her baby, they would have to kill her first. The community ordered her to leave the village with her son immediately, or they would kill them both. Today Richard travels the world as an advocate for people with disabilities and for other minority groups. He has dedicated his life to fighting for a just world.

I had goose bumps speaking with Richard. His passion and determination were unbelievable—they shone through him. I wondered what the people of his village would think if they could see him now.

The disability support group that he worked with currently only supported people with physical disabilities who were based in Kampala, but Richard gave us a list of other organisations to follow up with. Meeting him made me think about the word 'disability'. I didn't like how the word instantly focused on what someone was not able to do. When I was growing up, Mum had always said 'people with disabilities' rather than 'disabled people'. She always put the person before the disability. It wasn't just a matter of words; it was a way of thinking.

True to the shop's word, the next day the books were delivered to Namwendwa Primary School. The car driving down the track to the school created its own momentum, with some kids even chasing it along. When the car parked, the driver got out and began to unload box after box. The teachers gathered around and were squealing in delight. Then the boxes were torn open and each book was held high in the air with admiration. *So many beautiful new books*. With everyone's smiles and excitement, I had to try very hard not to cry. It was a very special moment.

The books were carefully placed on the shelves, every space being filled. Jane and I had also put the wall displays up, and would add the labels with the velcro when her parents arrived. *This really was a library now. Wow.*

It felt incredible to have had a vision and for everyone to have come together and transformed what was a dirty rat haven into a magnificent library. The school decided to open the library up to the community as well as the students so that everyone could enjoy and make use of this new resource. *Far out—it was exciting!*

●

Life was feeling so bright and amazing. I had a smile that felt glued to my face. And then a woman was murdered.

She was a young woman, only 20 years old, a mere two years older than myself. She lived in a house near the trading centre and we walked past her place most days. For reasons we didn't know—maybe for no reason at all—her husband macheted her to death. He literally chopped her into pieces. It was horrifying and brutal.

I wondered whether her husband would end up in the prison cell that I had encountered in the police station in Jinja, but Andrew told me he had already taken off. He said the man had probably paid off the local police not to chase him. It was very, very disturbing. But perhaps what I found most sickening was the community's reaction. The woman's mutilated body had been put on display in the trading centre for people to go and view. At the schools the teachers were joking and laughing about her death. I couldn't believe it—how could they make a mockery of this?

It felt very strange to be surrounded by people to whom death was so familiar. The reality was that people here were always dying. That was why families had so many children—they didn't anticipate that many of them would actually survive past the age of five. I realised that the laughter and light-heartedness that the community were showing was a coping mechanism. People still needed to farm their land if they were going to feed their family that night. The teachers still needed to go to work because they couldn't afford to miss a day.

I suddenly appreciated the sadness I felt. I was grateful for the tears that clouded my vision, and the horrific images that crowded my mind and haunted my dreams. They reminded me that death was not familiar to me. I had sufficient time and money to afford to be upset. It was strange to realise that everything I felt, positive or negative, was a luxury.

I also remembered my earlier thoughts concerning values. Perhaps family, friends and community were valued so strongly here because everyone profoundly understood how easily all these could all be taken away. *God, it felt like a catch 22.* Do we really have to lose the most important things in our lives for us to realise how meaningful they are?

Shit, it was science. It was Einstein's theory of relativity— you have to know cold to know hot, fast to know slow... Did we need to know death then to truly know life? This was obviously what people meant when they said poor people seem happy. Poor people appreciate what they have. But I still didn't like that saying. I wanted to lock these thoughts and feelings inside me. I wanted to realise and appreciate all the special people and things in my life while I still had them.

●

Jane and I spent a weekend away with some other female international volunteers. We visited the Murchison Falls, which were magnificent. Breathtakingly beautiful. We walked around the top and were so close to them that water sprayed onto our hot skin, refreshing both body and soul. I held my arms out like a bird about to take flight and closed my eyes. I felt so alive.

We also went on a game drive, which was everything I imagined. We saw elephants and giraffes, and were even fortunate enough to come across an entire family of lions.

It was nice simply being away and relaxing. Sometimes I had weird feelings of wishing Luke was there, and had to remind myself multiple times that he was a dickhead. I guess that 'grand realisations' don't come with an automatic switch for your emotions.

Jane and I got back to Namwendwa on the Monday afternoon to find the house a pigsty and notes from Wemusa and Lillian. They had both gone away—Wemusa for two weeks and Lillian for an indefinite period. I was immediately aware that this left Jane and I alone together and I worried about how this would affect us.

Wemusa had also taken 100 000 shillings (about $60) of our SPW project money. It may not sound like much, but a teacher in Uganda earns roughly 30 000 shillings ($19) a month so it was actually a fortune. It would have been nice if he had at least offered us an explanation for his behaviour. *Should we tell SPW about him stealing it? Or wait and see what he says when he returns?* We really had no idea what to do.

Jane and I spent all of Monday afternoon and Tuesday morning cleaning the house. All the dishes were dirty; there were maggots in our rubbish bag and rats on our beds. It was disgusting. I expected as much from Wemusa, but not from Lillian.

We were feeling flat that night, but it was the kids who cheered us up. It was a beautiful evening, so we were eating dinner outside. We were sitting on the mat and Jane had just served us each up a large bowl of rice and beans. All of the children were around us and seemed to be in a particularly hyper mood. Mirimu was dancing around like crazy; her little head was bobbing around, trying to keep up with her body.

Suddenly she stumbled and went face first into Jane's bowl of beans. When she pulled her face out and plonked herself down on the ground, she was a complete mess. At first, she went to stand up and resume her dancing, but Jane dashed inside and grabbed some toilet paper to try to clean her face. Only when Jane went to wipe the bean mess off Mirimu's cheeks did Mirimu seem to realise that she had it all over her face. She stood still, wide-eyed in horror. Her mouth then dropped open, ready for a full-blown wail. But Victoria started giggling, and we all followed suit. So, instead of crying, Mirimu laughed too, and I poured half my beans into Jane's bowl.

After dinner we were playing with the kids and I realised that whenever Kisashi spoke any English, she had an Australian accent. She sounded just like me! It was pretty hilarious to hear an Aussie twang from a young girl in a rural Ugandan village. I almost felt bad for her—I thought the Ugandan accent was much nicer than my one.

While Wemusa and Lillian remained absent, Jane and I kept ourselves busy by working to organise a Community Outreach Program. The master plan was to run the program over three days in separate rural areas throughout Namwendwa. We wanted to have counsellors and doctors available for HIV testing and also to have representatives from health and disability support NGOs. The objective of the program was to provide the community with opportunities to access more information about health issues and disabilities, to offer free counselling and HIV testing, and for relevant organisations to be present for people to make connections with them for ongoing support.

We needed to provide transport costs so that all the NGOs could attend. We also needed to pay the counsellors and doctors. On top of this, we needed to be able to provide everyone who attended with a free lunch as an incentive for them to put off working their land for the day. This meant that we needed to employ a cook, buy a whole lot of rice and beans, and thousands of small plastic bags in which the lunch would be served, as we had no hope of finding that many plates or bowls.

The budget for the program was $600, but SPW would only give us $150. They wouldn't have even given us that if they had known our last funds had gone walkabout with Wemusa. I had written home to everyone and every club that I could possibly think of, in the hope of getting the funds we needed donated.

Jane and I were sitting out the front of our house on the woven mat making our plans when we noticed that a lot of secondary school students were passing us, especially girls. It was too early for them to have finished all their lessons. We greeted the girls as they passed and asked why they were on their way home already. The girls said that they had been sent home because they had not paid the school fees for the new term.

Poverty means lack of choice, I thought. These girls did not have a choice about whether they received an education. Their parents didn't have a choice about how they spent their days—they either farmed their land or they went hungry. Life here was based around survival. People didn't even get to make simple choices like what to eat or what to wear, because what was available was so limited.

Something that I had learnt since being in this village was that no matter who you are one choice we always have is how we react to things. People here made the most of everything they had. I *really* admired that.

I found myself crying again. I only had three weeks of my placement left, three weeks left in Namwendwa. I had so much respect and love for this place and these amazing people. I tried to think about my experience of family life in Australia—hot showers, doona covers, fresh vegetables, muesli, chocolate . . . But as I sat out on the woven mat, with Jane beside me, and the children across the road playing, and the sun smiling down on us, all I really thought was: *I'm home. Right here, I'm home.*

10
The Hardest Thing

**NAMWENDWA, UGANDA—ADELAIDE, AUSTRALIA,
August 2005**

I was lying in Jinja backpackers, bored out of my brains. Jane's parents had arrived in Uganda and were visiting Namwendwa today. I didn't want to be there for it. I was afraid that if I were there I would spend the whole time feeling jealous and wishing my parents could visit too.

So here I was in Jinja. It was the middle of the week, so the hostel was dead. I didn't have anything much to do, so I spent the day eating and browsing the internet. The good news was that I had received positive responses from my emails and requests for donations from back in Australia for our planned Community Outreach Program. A Rotary Club offered to donate $400, and a Zonta club donated $200. This covered our complete budget, including providing transport for NGOs to attend and run workshops, paying counsellors and doctors to conduct HIV testing, buying rice and beans, and employing cooks for the days so we could offer everyone lunch.

I was pretty stoked. We had already received $150 from SPW but now we wouldn't need those funds for this program. We would be able to use their money to partially cover what Wemusa had stolen. That gave us time to wait for his possible explanation before deciding whether we dobbed him in or not. If he actually came back, that was.

•

Today was the big day. Day One of our Community Outreach Program, which we were hosting at Namwendwa Primary School. Jane's parents were in Kenya by now, Wemusa was yet to return and Lillian was back, but she had seriously annoyed me this morning. Jane and I had been ready at the primary school at 9 a.m., but Lillian remained in bed.

I was close to tears when we arrived at the school and found that nothing was set up. Andrew and Moses were there, but none of the other teachers were present. Nor were any of the counsellors, doctors or organisations that we had specifically requested to arrive early.

Andrew could obviously see the worry written all over my face. When I approached, he was quick to tell me that students were busy collecting benches from the classrooms. And then, as if on cue, primary students dressed in their bright pink T-shirts began carrying the wooden benches from their classrooms to the empty dirt space in front of the rooms. Students also brought benches from St Peter's, and a semicircle of benches began to take shape. This would be where the community would sit to watch the performances by the invited organisations such as TASO (The AIDS Support Organisation).

Outside this semi-circle, wooden tables and chairs were placed in little hubs. These would be the stations for precounselling, HIV testing and post-counselling. As the young students were racing about, rearranging the chairs at Andrew's direction, a ute rolled into the school grounds. On the back was the generator and PA system that we had hired from a store in Kamuli. At least someone had shown up on time.

The day had been scheduled to start at 10 a.m.; but by then we only had three community members present, and none of the counsellors, doctors or TASO people had yet arrived. The benches were alarmingly empty. I was running about like a headless chicken, holding my mobile phone high in the air and hoping desperately for at least a single bar of reception. During the brief moments when I had any flicker of opportunity, I quickly called each of the organisations that were supposed to have turned up an hour ago. They all laughed at my concerns and promised me that they were on their way.

'This is Africa' was the classic excuse, as if all the problems of the continent could forever justify being horribly late. Yes, there were endless problems in this continent and, yes, I was sure that sometimes such problems could contribute to lateness. But always? No, that was just ridiculous. And this is what I told TASO and the other organisations when at 11 a.m. they had still not shown up and I had rung them for the fourth time.

There was nothing left for us to do but sit and nervously wait, and hope that everyone would eventually show up. Slowly but surely they did. Lillian rocked up at about midday, and everyone else seemed to follow suit. People from the community seemed to appear suddenly and within a matter of minutes our audience went from a handful of people to roughly 600.

When the counsellors and doctors finally arrived, they set up immediately and began working. The community was responsive to the opportunity to be tested for HIV and there seemed to be a constant stream of people moving through the stages of counselling and having blood samples taken. It was a unique chance for them having these support organisations available, so they could make instant contact if they needed to.

Just when I was about to call TASO for the fifth time, they arrived. They entered on the back of a cattle truck and were chanting and drumming hand-held bongos. The women were wearing grass skirts that tossed wildly about as they danced to the rhythm. Instantly they got the community's attention, and people jumped up from the wooden benches and cheered at their spectacular arrival. A grin stretched across my face, and it no longer mattered that they were three hours late.

With TASO now here, and the HIV testing well underway, the official program for the day commenced. Moses was acting as MC and he greeted everyone enthusiastically. Then he invited the children from Florence's infants school to come forward and sing a welcoming song. Florence guided the tiny children, dressed in their smart blue uniforms, to the front of the semi-circle. They stood proudly and sang their well-rehearsed 'You Are Welcome' song. They then went on to sing a famous Ugandan song called 'AIDS is a Killer Disease'. With their young, sweet innocence the children sang: '*AIDS is a killer disease/Wherever you go, people are dying/They are mourning, they are burying, because of the killer disease.*' As the children sang, they acted out mourning (burying their heads in their hands) and then burying (making shovelling motions).

I had heard this song many times before, such as at our initial training, but it was a different experience hearing it now. It was extremely bizarre to watch five-year-olds sing about death with the same enthusiasm that a child in Australia might sing 'Twinkle Twinkle Little Star'. Of course it was only strange for Jane and myself. To everyone else, the performance was normal. The community loved it—they clapped loudly for the children, applauding their excellent singing and acting.

Next, Moses introduced Sam. As the headmaster of Namwendwa Primary, Sam was required to give an official welcoming and make an opening speech for the day's events. Formality is always insisted upon in Uganda, but I don't really like it. Sam did though, because it gave him an excuse to talk—and he loved the sound of his own voice.

Sam's speech started as expected, with him enthusiastically welcoming everyone and emphasising the significance of the day and the importance of health awareness. He somehow stretched this spiel over ten minutes and, just as I thought he must be near ready to hand back the microphone, he suddenly started talking about condoms. *Oh dear, where is this going?!* He pointed to his genitals and then declared that African men are big. He went on to say that many feared that condoms would break if they used them, because they weren't made for African men. *Oh shit, please stop talking.*

I looked frantically at Moses, who was by now standing awkwardly behind Sam while trying to encourage him to give the mic back. But Sam was not finished yet. I looked around at the community members and wondered how much they could understand as Sam was speaking in English, rather than Lusoga. What Sam did next though transcended any language barrier—he pulled a condom out of his pocket and proceeded to blow it up. The condom now looked like a penis balloon and Sam held it smugly above his head. 'But unless you are bigger than this,' he let out a satisfied little laugh, 'it will fit you!'

And then he handed the mic back to Moses, and went and sat down. I certainly hadn't anticipated that little exhibition, but I had to admit it was kind of brilliant.

Moses then got the program back on track, and all the organisations gave excellent speeches or performances. But TASO was definitely the highlight. They performed a role-play that demonstrated how to care for someone with HIV/AIDS; someone gave an informative talk; and someone else, who was HIV infected, provided a personal testimony. Everything was in Lusoga, so it was completely accessible to the community, and everyone seemed extremely engaged the entire time.

The official program concluded at roughly 4 p.m., by which time I was starving. Andrew had insisted that we could not serve lunch until the program was complete. He said otherwise people would simply eat and leave.

We had employed two cooks for the day and bought huge amounts of rice and beans. A middle-aged woman and man prepared the food over two large charcoal stoves. When I peered at the boiling pots, it didn't exactly look appetising but I was so hungry. Also, compared to *porcho*, rice was a luxury.

There were over 600 mouths to feed but everyone lined up patiently for a plastic bag with a scoop of rice and beans. With their sweating bags, people happily returned to the benches and used their hands to indulge in the provided feast.

●

We hosted days two and three of the program in Namwendwa's neighbouring communities. Given the program contained life-saving information, as well as the opportunity to be HIV tested, we wanted to reach as many people as possible. Days two and three turned out to be very similar to the first day of the program, except that I wasn't so stressed. When people were two hours late, I expected it and it was no longer a problem. Something that really impressed me, however, was that the teachers from Namwendwa Primary School helped us set up and run the program, even when it was in a different area. I realised that the value of community here extended beyond any village parameters. Life was just better when everyone worked together.

When Wemusa returned home he had a new watch. *Hmm, I wonder how he got the money for that,* I thought sarcastically. He also returned with malaria. Since coming back, he hadn't moved from his bed, but that wasn't exactly anything different for him. Perhaps I should have felt sorry for him, but you become a bit immune to words like 'malaria' when everyone around you seems to have it all the time. It would be like someone in Australia telling me they had a cold. Except, obviously, malaria is life-threatening. It was astounding how easy it was to forget that.

I couldn't help thinking that it was quite convenient for Wemusa to have malaria—it would make Jane and I seem horrible if we now questioned him about the money. Perhaps I was nasty anyway for doubting his honesty and querying whether he had malaria at all, but history showed I had every good reason to be wary of him.

Jane and I did not have much time left in the village by now. As we started to get organised to leave Namwendwa, we decided that we wanted to set up something ongoing to support the community. We asked the teachers and other people what they thought might be a good idea. Everyone wanted to empower females and felt that the most effective way to do this was through education. Male enrolment consistently outnumbered female enrolment at the secondary school. The teachers suggested that we set up a sponsorship program with acceptance criteria based on academic merit, rather than a needs basis. Everyone was in equal need.

Jane and I decided to set up a scholarship program as the teachers and community had recommended. We would sponsor eight girls from Namwendwa Primary School to attend St Peter's Secondary School. These were the two schools at which we had taught, and where we had the connections. The girls would be selected based on their exam results in their final year of primary school. Jane would cover the cost of four of the scholarships, and I would also fund four. We figured that even if no-one at home supported us we would be able to afford this amount.

The girls were selected while we were there, and we gave them letters of congratulations and took their photographs. The girls were so excited! We arranged to transfer funds for each year of their education through an organisation in Kamuli. It felt good to be able to offer them and the community something special. The scholarship program would hopefully not only provide the opportunity of education for the selected girls, but also help females generally to feel recognised and empowered in the general community.

Soon we had only one week left in Namwendwa and so Jane and I decided to work out which of our possessions we would be leaving behind—clothes, stationery, cooking items and so on. We organised these into individual piles and gave them to each of the families that we were closest with. I felt a little bit funny choosing people to give my belongings to, but I knew it would have felt weirder to return home with these things simply because I was afraid of being unfair.

The families were very grateful for these gifts and all insisted on giving us something in return. We received so many groundnuts! The kids had a ball dressing up in our old clothes and parading them back and forth. I gave one of my skirts to Kisashi—now she had an outfit to match her Aussie accent. I gave my nicest skirt and top to Kigali. Her mother put the clothes on her and she was gentle and kind. It was heartwarming to see her acting in such a loving and caring way toward her daughter. Kigali was now being treated like the special, beautiful girl she was. Maybe if people in the community started to see this shift in Kigali's family, it would start a ripple effect. I truly hoped so.

I wished that I had been able to organise another Community Outreach Program based on raising awareness about what it means to have an intellectual or physical disability and having support organisations available. But the days had flown by like pretty birds and disappeared into the blue sky. And I was left feeling like I never had enough time.

After visiting the families, Jane and I walked up to Florence's infants school. Florence was so excited to see us, but her happiness turned to concern when she realised we were there to say goodbye. I gave Florence a big hug, and then gave her my mobile phone. Given there was now a phone tower right next to her house, it felt only right for Florence to be able to make use of it. It also meant that we would always be able to stay in touch. Florence was so excited by the gift that she was jumping up and down while clapping her hands. Jane and I each hugged her again, and then turned back down the dirt path to return home.

It was heartwarming visiting each family, playing with the kids and especially saying goodbye to Florence. But afterwards the tears flowed. *How was I ever going to leave?*

●

Wemusa had by now recovered from malaria and was being suspiciously nice. He was obviously trying to win us over, in the hope that we wouldn't tell SPW he had stolen our project money and bought a watch. I wanted to tell SPW. Wemusa had no reason for stealing the money, and he had been inconsiderate and selfish for the past seven months. (With the exception of the week leading up to his birthday. What a coincidence! Not.)

Jane was unsure about saying anything to SPW. She raised the point that it wouldn't actually achieve or change anything if we did. Sometimes it was so hard, even impossible, to know what was the right thing to do. But before we knew it our very last day in Namwendwa arrived. The next morning at 6 a.m. a *matatu* would pick us up from our home and take us to Jinja, where we would meet up with all the other SPW volunteers for a debrief. Countless thoughts and feelings were racing through me that day—and there was plenty of tears. This place had become my home. These people had become my family and friends. And, unlike when

I left Australia, when or if I would ever return to this magical country was uncertain.

Both the primary and secondary schools put on separate parties for us, each involving a massive lunch and a little concert in our honour. It was overwhelming having so many special people in the same space, and the rarity of Lillian and Wemusa both being around made it all the more wonderful. Despite my mixed feelings toward Wemusa, he was part of my family here too. He and Lillian would also leave Namwendwa tomorrow, but of course it would only ever be a bus ride away for them. For Jane and me leaving was a lot more emotional.

My tears started when the Young Women's Group from the secondary school began singing 'AIDS is a Killer Disease'... What was it with this song?! Everyone loved it. The girls had such high-pitched voices that, if I hadn't already known the words off by heart, I would have had no idea what they were singing.

After the formalities and eating were over, it was time to say our farewells. I was a blubbering mess saying goodbye to Andrew and Moses. They asked me not to cry, but I couldn't help it.

Back at home we placed the few belongings we had retained into the bags we had first come with. My shiny-red, newly-purchased backpack had been basically unused while I had been here—it hadn't really been needed. I put my few clothes back into its capacious interior, along with all my diaries, a novel, my camera and the head torch that I had used every evening.

We pulled our pictures down off the walls. I held the photo of Josh for a moment, and smiled. There were reasons to go back to Australia. Mum, Dad and Josh had just recently got back there after their stint in Ireland. They were building a new house on Hindmarsh Island and in the meantime living in a small cottage in Goolwa, about an hour and a half out of Adelaide. My older brother Sam was living in a sharehouse in Adelaide. I had no idea where I would live on my return, but that still felt a world away.

After we packed up our things, we swept the house. It didn't take long. We had given away all our basins and pots, and the charcoal stove—only our four beds remained. It was back to looking like a house rather than a home. I couldn't handle seeing it this way, and escaped outside.

Jane and I played with the kids. At first it was mainly just some of the kids from across the road—Kisashi, Victoria and Mirimu. But as we held hands and jumped around in a circle singing in Lusoga, more kids came and joined in. I pulled off my brown sandals and let my feet twist and turn in the dirt. We raced around in a circle, each of us erupting into giggles as we bounced up and down.

In all the time I had been here, I still hadn't been able to work out if the words to the song actually made sense or were only a nonsense nursery rhyme. But either way, it didn't matter. I knew when I was supposed to bob up and down, and when I needed to run into the middle of the circle and throw my hands in the air.

There were lots of us playing now, maybe fifteen kids or so. I knew most of them by the sound of their laughter rather than their names. However, Dawoodee would not play. He watched from the nearby tree. He was probably only ten years old, but it was obvious that he felt too old for this game. I remembered how cool and grown up some of the boys had tried to act when I was in primary school. There were boys in Year Six smoking cigarettes and using the lingo of an 18-year-old. I had always wanted to tell them that being a kid was actually a lot of fun and that they were missing out. Of course, I never actually said that or I would have spent the rest of my schooling being bullied.

I tried to pull myself out of the group for a moment. Mirimu looked up at me and I had to uncurl her fingers that were clinging onto mine. I promised her that I would come back in a minute.

Dawoodee had his ball by his feet, and I went over and gestured for him to kick it. We kicked the ball back and forth. As the other kids saw what was happening, the singing stopped and instead a soccer game kicked off. None of us could keep up with Dawoodee, but we had a lot of fun trying.

We played until it was dark, and one by one the kids retreated back to their houses. Jane and I then returned to our room. Lillian and Wemusa were in their beds. I lay down. It was pitch black and my head torch was already packed. I rummaged through my bag, my hands feeling for its distinctive shape, and then I found it. I also unpacked my current diary.

Jane found her torch too and we lay, as we had done most nights, hidden under our nets, lights on and diaries out. I was too overwhelmed to write and instead lay on my back, pulling the strap of the torch from around my head and holding it in my hands. I shone the light over every detail of the room. There were so many cracks in the cement—lines that broke off into more lines. I felt absorbed by every detail—I wanted to lock it all away into my memory. It seemed that I needed to know, to be able to remember, every single thing, so that this place would always feel as real as it was to me right at this moment.

When Jane's light flickered off, and she wished me goodnight for the final time, I switched my own light off too. I lay awake. I didn't even know what I was thinking. I just knew how I felt, and I felt devastatingly sad.

●

Debrief was at a campsite next to the Nile river. It was a beautiful spot. When we arrived though, the place was swarming with people, certainly a lot more than had volunteered on our program. Jane, Wemusa, Lillian and I entered the chaos to discover that the debrief was also for a much larger group of Ugandan SPW volunteers who had all just done a one-month placement. I was pretty disappointed. I felt a need to discuss and reflect on all the experiences of the past eight months, but it was immediately clear that wasn't going to happen.

There was an area with tables and couches where we all ate dinner. It was a similar set-up to when we had been on training. Luke was with a new girl now. Apparently she was a UK volunteer from another program. It felt very strange watching him interact with her in the same way as he had done with me. It was also just peculiar that he had brought her here. *Who brings a date to debrief?*

Luke and his girlfriend disappeared after dinner. *Out of sight, out of mind*, I thought, *and now, after everything, out of my life.* I was disappointed but relieved to see him go. He probably thought I was just some fling—a foolish girl whom he had so easily strung along. But I supposed that, in a way, I had used him too—to help me let go of Jack. Or perhaps it was just easier for me to tell myself that was the only significance he had played in my life. But whatever he had or hadn't meant to me, now he was gone. Gone for good.

Jane too was leaving. She had to go to Uganda's international airport at Entebbe. She was flying to Kenya to meet up with her family for a holiday before returning to cold England. Jane and I said goodbye quite casually. We were probably too exhausted from our earlier farewells to be overly emotional now. And of course we planned to stay in contact—we still had the scholarship scheme tying us together.

Lindy had decided that she was sick of the debrief, so she headed for Kampala. This wasn't how I had expected this journey to end. It was all very anti-climactic. I went to bed early, feeling somewhat abandoned. The place was overrun with people I didn't know. This had been the last opportunity for all of us volunteers, both Ugandan and international, to be together, and now that moment was lost. It was also strange being able to reach my arms out of my bed into open space; I was so used to Jane being only inches away.

After breakfast in the morning, Irene asked to speak to me. *Oh god.* I had had little to do with Irene since our training, but I still felt uneasy around her. I followed her outside, where I spotted two wooden chairs facing each other. Irene sat in one and I sat opposite her. Then Paul appeared and stood behind her. *What was this all about?*

Irene didn't bother trying to make me feel comfortable; she seemed to crave power. She immediately questioned me about Lillian and Wemusa. She wanted to know how much time they had actually spent on placement. She wanted to know about how the SPW funds had been spent. She suggested to me that perhaps some of our funds had been misused.

Jane wasn't here now for me to turn to for answers, for an understanding of the right thing to say. I wondered what would happen if I told the truth—if I said Lillian was hardly around and if I admitted that Wemusa had stolen 100 000 shillings. Would they just talk to Lillian and Wemusa about it? That was what I imagined would happen in a similar scenario in Australia. But I didn't really know how things would be handled here. I especially didn't know how Irene would respond. She was such an odd character. I suspected that she actually had a really low self-esteem to be as controlling as she was, but that made her completely unpredictable.

I shuffled in my seat for a moment and then I said that Lillian sometimes went away on weekends, but that she was always around for our classes. I said that Wemusa and I didn't get along, but that he had always been on placement.

I said that we spent all our SPW funding as planned and beamed a little when I talked about the Community Outreach Program.

I lied. I wasn't really sure why I was lying. I didn't even like Wemusa, but I thought, *We are all who we are for a reason*. I knew Wemusa's dad had multiple wives and that Wemusa had a zillion siblings, but beyond that I didn't really know anything about him. Maybe if I did know more, there would be an explanation for his behaviour. It wasn't that I thought anything and everything was excusable. More to the point, I didn't know what I thought.

After I had finished my cosmetic little gloss, Irene gave a sly smile and announced that they already knew Lillian had another job and that Wemusa had taken the project money. *What?* Irene went on to tell me that they had forgiven Lillian and that Wemusa was going to pay the money back to the organisation in time.

I sat there stunned. She had interrogated me for nothing more than her own pleasure. She really did have issues. I had had enough. I stood up and walked away. It was a mystery to me how they knew everything. Then again, I did not have a very good poker face.

I no longer felt any need to stay at the debrief, and so I decided to leave. I walked straight to the dorm room I was in and grabbed my red pack. I said goodbye to Lillian, giving her a hug and promising to stay in touch. My farewell to Wemusa was a lot briefer—I was glad there was no forced display of emotion; neither of us mentioned the money situation.

I walked out of the campsite and onto the nearby road. *Buda-buda* men quickly encircled me and, after I had bartered for the best price, I clambered onto the back of a bike. I had my large backpack on and so I had to put my hands on the *buda-buda* man's waist to hold my balance.

This was it. I was going back to Kampala. Back to the airport in Entebbe. Back to Australia.

11
The Phone Call

ADELAIDE, AUSTRALIA, September 2005–June 2006

I walked into the arrivals hall at Adelaide airport, following the other passengers like a lemming. My mind was completely silent but I didn't feel like I had reached enlightenment. I felt empty.

And then, there they were—Mum, Dad and Josh. Dad recognised me first and had to point me out to Mum. She had been too busy looking out for the person with the red backpack, forgetting that I hadn't collected my luggage yet. I had flown home via Sydney, so this final leg of my journey had only been a domestic flight.

I walked over to them smiling, and gave Mum the first hug. She had sent me at least one letter every month while I had been away, including posting me word puzzles and sudokus, even though she knew I didn't like anything with numbers. She had also sent me parcels with marshmallows to roast and many other goodies too. She was the most thoughtful person I knew. She cried when we hugged; she was so excited to see me. I could feel her warmth.

Next I hugged Dad. We had only spoken once while I was away, which was when I rang to ask how many laxatives I could take without doing damage. The box had said two; Dad said as many as it took to do the job. It came in handy having a doctor for a dad and I ended up taking twelve. I had been expecting something pretty grand to follow, and was disappointed when I produced nothing more than a pellet. But at least it was something.

It was a little awkward hugging Dad. I had spent my last year of school resenting him for leaving our family for his Antarctic adventure. It was a time when I had felt we really needed him around, but he hadn't been. I had told him this many times and he had become defensive, arguing that he was working there. This was true, but there were plenty of jobs in Adelaide. While I had been away I had forgiven him for leaving, as I felt that there are things that as individuals we just need to do. For me, it was going to Uganda; for Dad, perhaps it was Antarctica. This was a thought that I should have vocalised, but I never did.

When Dad stopped patting my back, I realised the hug was over and I turned to Josh. He was happy to have me back and was singing his version of 'We Are Family', *I've got my sister with me . . .'* I laughed, and took his hand. I asked him to help me get my bag.

My older brother, Sam, hadn't come to the airport. He had to work that day.

It was all a bit surreal. I looked at the moving ground beside me—a travelator—totally ridiculous. But, of course, Josh wanted us to run along it, and to race Mum and Dad as they walked with only their legs to carry them. I let Josh pull me onto it, jumping off my moral high-horse and chasing my little brother.

I collected my red pack and mocked Mum by asking her if I was now more recognisable. Josh and I followed her and Dad out to the car. It was a typical winter's afternoon, wet and cold. Mum, Dad and Josh were all in jeans and jumpers. I was wearing a red skirt that I had had tailor-made in Jinja from some material I had found in Kamuli, and a black tank top. In other words, I was freezing. The ludicrous thing was that I had actually put a lot of thought into my airport outfit. I had wanted to wear something flattering, but which also reflected Africa and my time away. *What a tourist!* I hadn't even considered the weather. My stupidity had plummeted to a whole new nadir.

We raced to the car. I lagged behind, blaming my pack for weighing me down. Josh yelled at the sky for being naughty—he didn't appreciate getting wet.

It was an hour and a half's drive to their cottage in Goolwa. Dad drove, Mum sat in the front, Josh and I in the back, with my bag in the boot. I was a little envious of my bag, because

I felt like hiding away. I couldn't be bothered with small talk. Mum was firing me with questions, all in the name of motherly love; but I was just not in the zone. *Yes*, the flights were good. *No*, they weren't too long (I was lying now, but it was only a white lie). *Yes,* they had served me vegetarian food . . .

I gazed out the window. Through the rain I watched a slideshow of buildings. I wasn't really here. I wasn't sure where I was but it wasn't here, in this car with the heating, my brother singing, and my mum twisting in her seat to give me concerned looks.

As we drew nearer to their cottage, Josh's hunger was growing and he asked at least ten times what was for dinner. Dad suggested that we get a pizza. Suddenly I was in the moment and my mouth was salivating a little. Perhaps a lot. It was the cheese in particular that I was craving. Without electricity in Namwendwa, refrigeration had been impossible to come by, which meant that I had had few dairy products while away. *Mmmmm, cheese*.

We stopped for pizza. Fortunately it had stopped raining, and I stood by the open boot, rummaging through my bag for a jumper. Then I remembered that I had given almost all my clothes away but I had kept my lightweight rain jacket, so I put that on.

The pizza place was primarily a takeaway joint but had a few tables with chairs around them, so we took a seat. Mum did the ordering, and Josh kept us entertained while we waited. Once the pizza arrived, we wasted no time in diving in. The cheese was good, the mushrooms and olives were also a treat, and I didn't even used to like olives.

WE ARE ONE VILLAGE

After annihilating the pizza in about five minutes, we were on the road again. It was dark when we arrived at the cottage. I followed my family into their temporary home. The cottage had two bedrooms, a small lounge room, a tiny kitchen and a laundry. Josh's room had bunk beds. Josh had always chosen to sleep on the bottom one when we'd been like this before, and so I clambered up onto the top bunk. It was nice to have Josh so close, but at the same time I immediately thought that there was not room for me in this place. That thought was a little ironical, given the shoebox home that I had shared in Uganda. I supposed that whether I liked it or not, I had in-built expectations of how things should be here.

I thought of the beautiful room that I had had in our family home. It had been so spacious and light. As I stared into the dark now, I realised that, while I had thought about leaving the family home, I never considered that I wouldn't actually live with my family again. I wondered if they had thought about that when they moved into this place. Bunking with Josh was obviously only a temporary solution—I needed to find somewhere to live.

Mum popped her head in to say goodnight and then she said, 'Welcome home.'

I replied with '*Sula burungi*' and then explained to Mum that it meant goodnight in Lusoga. Then, as she disappeared and Josh started snoring, I turned to face the wall, closed my eyes and dreamt of Namwendwa.

●

I woke and was a little shocked to find myself elevated. It took me a moment to remember that I was in Mum and Dad's cottage and that I had slept in Josh's top bunk. I peered over the side of the bed to see if Josh was still asleep. His covers were dishevelled at the end of his mattress, and he was nowhere to be seen.

I might not have been able to see him, but I could hear him. He was nattering away in the room next door. Was that the kitchen or the lounge? I couldn't remember.

Urgh. I did not feel good. I recalled once seeing a comedian on TV who had made a joke about how Australians talk, commenting on how we love the word 'not'. *How far is the pub?* Not far. *How do you feel?* Not bad. *How much does that cost?* Not much. The memory made me smile, as I sat up in bed, feeling *not good*. I felt gross for multiple reasons. Firstly, because I had slept in the same clothes that I had been wearing for the last two days. But on top of my lack of hygiene and uncomfortable outfit, my stomach was also churning. I decided I was hungry, even though I knew I was lying to myself. I was just excited to indulge in the goodness of muesli.

I climbed down from the top bunk and wandered into the next room, which wasn't the kitchen or the lounge, but rather the dining area. I found Mum, Dad and Josh sitting around the table. Josh was chowing down bacon and eggs on toast, and he had tomato sauce smeared all over his face. He glanced up when he heard me enter; he quickly swallowed his mouthful, said hello, and was then head down, food in mouth once more.

Mum and Dad didn't seem nearly as excited by their breakfast. Dad was slowly eating a bowl of cereal while reading the newspaper. And Mum was pausing between every mouthful to have a sip of her tea. She was possibly a tea addict.

Mum pulled a funny face when she saw me. She didn't need to say anything; her down-turned mouth and raised eyebrows were already questioning me: *Oh Nikki,* her expression exclaimed, *did you sleep in that?*

I said good morning to my family and then explained that I had been so tired that I had slept in my clothes. I thought I would save Mum the trouble of having to actually ask me, and it clearly worked because, after my explanation, her eyebrows seemed to relax a little. She led me into the kitchen to show me where the breakfast things were. I almost did a little dance when she pulled a tub of berry yoghurt out of the fridge. Yummo! I filled my bowl with muesli and yoghurt despite my stomach gurgling in protest.

After my delicious breakfast, I should have been happy and satisfied but my guts were having an absolute fit. I dashed to the toilet and the contents of my intestines exploded out of me. Diarrhoea. *Gross.* I sat on the toilet disgusted, but I couldn't help thinking the whole situation was a little ironic. I had spent eight months drinking bore water and eating street food in a place where stomach bugs were rife and yet I had been constipated for most of the time. Now, after one night in Australia, here I was stuck on the toilet for the opposite reason. I buried my head in my hands as my intestines continued to churn.

Once I was convinced that there was nothing left to come out, I returned to the dining area. But my family were no longer there. Josh had returned to his room and was singing and dancing to some pop song I didn't know. I found Mum out the front, pottering about in the small garden. And Dad had apparently gone out. I stood by the door to the cottage, watching Mum happily tend to the plants. Everyone was busy doing their thing, and I had nothing to do. No projects to plan; no charcoal stove that needed lighting or water that needed to be fetched; no rats to chase or toads to sweep away; no kids across the road to play with; no Jane to gossip with . . . just me.

Before I went to Uganda, all my time had been consumed by school and Jack. Now I didn't have them either. I didn't even have a bedroom.

Mum noticed me, posed like a statue by the door, and asked if I was okay. I told her that I was a little lost, so she suggested that I call a friend. I used her mobile and dialled the number of my old school friend Lisa. She was thrilled to hear my voice and know that I was back in Australia. It was a Friday; she and some of the other girls that I knew from school were going out to town that night. Lisa begged for me to join them, and offered for me to crash at her place for the next few nights. I had only just turned eighteen when I left for Uganda, so I had never actually been to an Australian club before. I was rapt at the idea of being consumed by music and dance.

I asked Lisa to wait a sec, then raced to the front garden again and asked Mum if there was a bus to get to town. Mum told me that there was and that it would drop me at Marion Shopping Centre. I asked Lisa if she could pick me up from there and she laughed; she couldn't believe I was even asking—of course she would pick me up.

I had a flickering moment of feeling like a typical teenager as I thought, *What on earth am I going to wear?* I raced out to Mum and told her my dilemma. As always, she knew what to do and popped inside to grab the car keys. We were soon cruising along to the storage shed where all my belongings were stashed. It was bizarre to see my old life in boxes.

After I left for Uganda, Mum and Dad had sold our family home and boxed everything into storage. They had got their stuff back when they returned from Ireland, but my things remained packed away. Mum was very organised and had labelled each carton of my belongings in clear black texta. I quickly found my clothes box and packed it into the car. I didn't need any of my other stuff yet; besides, I had nowhere to put anything. Back at the cottage I went through my clothes, shoved a few into a small backpack of Josh's and caught the bus to town.

It was exciting to meet up with Lisa. I gave her a hug and her first comment was about how brown I was. She asked me about my trip, but it was impossible to summarise my experience, so I simply said it was good. I had already realised that no-one really wanted to know the details of my time away, maybe because it was too far removed, too difficult for them to imagine. Or perhaps it was because that was all in the past now, and everyone was more concerned with the future.

It was strange that evening to go through the motions of getting ready for a night out. I had a hot shower, and Lisa curled my hair and prettied my face with make-up. I slipped into my dress, and barely recognised the girl in the mirror. We met up with some other girls and caught the train into town. There was only a handful of people on the train and I appreciated having space to breathe. We had a lot of fun that night, drinking and giggling, flirting with boys, and dancing until our feet hurt.

Lisa's brother picked us up later and drove us back to their house. Lisa and I laughed the whole way, and back at her place we ate ice-cream before crawling into bed and reminiscing about the night that had been.

The weeks passed and I seemed to fall into a routine of drinking and dancing. Lisa became my partner in crime. But then, as though someone had flicked a switch inside me, the novelty of going out was gone. I moved out of Lisa's house and into my aunty's place. She and her two daughters shared a house with her partner, and they had a spare room. They offered for me to stay there; it was only meant to be a temporary arrangement.

After I moved in, I decided that I needed a job and found one immediately working for a marketing company to promote the aid organisation Save the Children. I started work the next day at 7 a.m. I was one of those annoying people in shopping centres, stationed at a table in the middle of the mall itself, calling out 'Can I ask you a quick question?' I was the person that everyone wanted to avoid. I worked six days a week, 12 hours a day, trying to convince myself I was doing something worthwhile.

When the switch went off inside me, it wasn't just the novelty of going out that I lost. I stopped enjoying hot showers, nice food, my soft doona; I didn't even like flushing the toilet. Everything felt wasteful and over-indulgent. I felt constant guilt. As if to flush out such shame, my diarrhoea also continued. I discovered that while I had been away my body had become intolerant to dairy foods.

I was always thinking of Namwendwa. I spoke at all the different Rotary, Lions and Zonta clubs that had been supportive of our efforts there, and every time I presented I would become overwhelmed with sadness and not be able to control my tears. People were moved by my passion, and clubs as well as individuals offered to sponsor a girl's education through the scholarship program that Jane and I had initiated. As difficult as I found talking about it, I liked how it connected me back to the community in Uganda, and how it also then connected others.

I often tried talking to Mum about my feelings. The three of them were still living in the cottage and sometimes I would visit, but it seemed like almost every evening would end with me in tears. One particular night over dinner, after seeing a news story on child abuse, we were talking about it and I suddenly remembered the little boy from Namwendwa Primary School who had been thrown on the ground and whipped repeatedly by a teacher. His story was not unique. The memory caused me to erupt into tears, and I raced into Josh's room and leaned against the bottom bunk. I wrapped my arms around my knees, pulling them into my chest. I was rocking back and forth against this bed that was not mine. Tears were flowing uncontrollably and my head was pounding.

Mum came and sat beside me; she pulled my body in tight and tried to stop my shaking. She begged for me to talk to her and I could sense her worry. I broke away from her grasp and for the first time I realised exactly how I felt. I looked her in the eyes and asked her how she would feel if she knew I was starving, if she knew that Josh could never go to school, if she knew that Dad had a life-threatening illness.

I could see her eyes filling with tears. I didn't want to hurt her. I was just trying to explain how I felt every day. I told Mum that the families and the friends and the community of people I loved back in the village were not okay. Mum was crying now too. She pulled me into her again, and we sat in silent sadness. Finally she whispered that she didn't know what to say. And I sighed, replying that I didn't know what to do.

●

I continued to live at my aunty's house and distracted myself by working long hours until university started in March 2006. Then I commenced a degree in Journalism and International Studies. I had actually only applied for the course because at the time it had the highest TER and my plan had been not to be accepted. It seemed easier to say that I hadn't got into my chosen course, rather than to admit that I wasn't sure I even wanted to go to uni. But then, to my surprise, I was accepted and everyone expected that I would go. My supposed gap year was over and now, apparently, it was time to get on with life. It seemed contradictory to me that it was a called a gap year when in fact it was the most full-on year of my life; I was sure I had learnt more in that short time than I ever had at school or would at uni.

I spent my days at uni lying on the grass and imagining pictures within the clouds. I rarely went to class. I watched other students rushing about, studying hard, eager to please. Other girls seemed to float around the campus; they always looked so light and lovely. They gossiped and giggled, and were absorbed in their own world. I watched them closely, not with disgust but with jealousy. Ignorance was bliss, I thought.

The only class I did enjoy was Spanish, which was an elective as part of the International Studies degree. After my first Spanish class, a boy with curly hair and vibrant blue eyes approached me. His name was Tom and he said that he had overheard me talking to someone else, and was curious to know about the time I had spent in Uganda. He genuinely seemed to want to know all about my experience. He told me that he himself had spent the last year volunteering in Peru; he also told me he was a musician. I asked him if he would bring me a CD of his music, and he asked if I would bring him the Lonely Planet book in which I had first found out about SPW's work in Uganda.

The next week we both brought our items to exchange and, as easily as that, our friendship was sealed. Tom was an intriguing character—while most guys wore polo shirts or trendy brands, he wore daggy jeans, woollen old-man vests and black fingerless gloves. He was anything but conventional. Over the months that followed, Tom and I shared our stories about far-away places. I went to his gigs and met his friends. While I still felt adrift at uni, I was starting to build a life for myself. I was beginning to feel a lot more at ease and a lot happier. On one particular day, Tom turned up to Spanish late and, when he came in and sat beside me, he looked remarkably different. He had shaved his facial hair and cut his hair. He looked . . . *attractive*. We had been friends for a while now and never once had it occurred to me that Tom was good looking, but he was. It was weird, and I tried to push the thoughts to the back of my head.

Most nights I lay in bed, restlessly thinking of Namwendwa, but that night I found myself thinking of Tom. He really did look different. The thought of him must have brought me at least temporary peace, because sleep overcame me.

When I woke, it was pitch dark and my phone was ringing. In my scattered, half-asleep state, my hand felt around for my phone. But then the ringing stopped. I gave up searching for my phone and closed my eyes again. Just as I did, the ringing began once more, and then it stopped. Someone was pranking me. I was tempted to ignore it; sleep was summoning me. I closed my eyes and pulled the pillow over my head. The phone rang again. This time curiosity got the better of me, and I jumped up and flicked on a nearby lamp.

I found my phone beside the mattress. Three missed calls—Florence! Florence was pranking me. I hadn't spoken to her for months and any frustration about being woken disappeared, so I called her back immediately. I was so excited at hearing her voice, but my body froze when she answered. She was in hysterics.

'Florence, Florence, what's wrong?'

It was extremely difficult to understand her—it was a bad line, fuzzy with long delays, and the howling of her cries was draining out her words.

I asked her again, 'Florence, what's wrong?'

Finally I understood what she was saying—termites had destroyed the infants school. She was trying to teach out of her single-room home, but of course there was not enough space. She didn't know what to do. But finally I did.

I promised to help.

12
Catch 22

ADELAIDE, AUSTRALIA, July 2006–January 2007

I was restless, and couldn't sleep. I was back in my room at my aunty's house. My temporary moving in had now stretched to over six months; my aunty Sharon was kind for being so generous with her home. I liked it here.

I was lying in bed, wondering how on earth I was going to do all that I had promised. I had spoken to Florence many times over the past few weeks. I had asked her to get a quote for constructing a two-bedroom brick building for the infants school. Initially she had thought it would only cost a few thousand dollars, but now it seemed like it might be much more. I had no idea how I was going to come up with the money.

I felt stressed on the time front as well. With uni, my part-time job back at the bakery (I was already saving for a return trip to Uganda) and, well, socialising, I was already almost constantly busy even before I first spoke to Florence. Now I felt overwhelmed—there were people reliant on me. *Me!* That was a scary thought.

I hated lying in bed and wishing that I were asleep, so I decided just to get up instead. It was the middle of the night and everyone else was out to it. I crept past my little cousins' rooms and into the kitchen, got myself a large bowl of muesli and then snuck into the back room. I sat on the couch and turned on the TV. There was a lot of rubbish and, as I flicked through the stations, I was beginning to think it was more entertaining lying in bed staring into blackness. But then I switched to SBS, and my heart nearly stopped. The program was on HIV/AIDS and a thin woman with a British accent was interviewing people from TASO in Uganda. I couldn't believe it. I put my bowl on a nearby table and sat right in front of the TV. Suddenly I recognised one of the women on the screen. She was the same woman who had given a testimonial at our training—the woman whose husband had died of AIDS and who was now infected. I knew her; I knew her story.

My tears came uncontrollably and I couldn't even pinpoint what it was in particular that was so upsetting. I sat with my face right in front of the screen until the program finished and then I turned the TV off. The room was silent.

I had known the woman they interviewed, but the program had reminded me of someone else. It made me think about Harriet and the day that I had taken her and the four other girls to be HIV tested. I remembered how terrified she had been that day, how her whole body had been shaking. But, unbelievably, Harriet had not been afraid for herself—she had been anxious for her family. She was worried about the impact that it would have on them if she were HIV infected. She was so selfless and so brave. She had been petrified, but she chose to be tested anyway because of the value she placed on her family. I admired her so much.

As my mind relived that moment with Harriet, I also recalled that I had visited Florence that day. I had been exhausted, but she had been her normal excited self. She had told me all her plans for the infants school. *God—maybe there are no coincidences.* Harriet had shown me what it meant to be truly courageous and Florence had shared with me her dream. Tonight, when I had been so full of self-doubt, this program just happened to be on at the very time that I couldn't sleep and I just happened to turn on the TV in the middle of the night. And now this documentary had brought me back to Namwendwa. It had reminded me of women who I admired so strongly—Harriet, Florence and also Jane. And remembering these women and that particular day, I recalled the values that I found embraced in Uganda—family, friends and community.

I smiled to myself: *I will find a way to raise this money.* One birthday when I was young, my parents had given me a card; on its cover had been a small child wearing over-sized red boxing gloves with a punching bag high above his head. The card read: 'If you can dream it, you can do it. Dream big.'

I was wide awake now and I jumped onto the computer that was also in the back room. I began typing fundraising ideas—movie nights, quiz nights, street BBQs, music festivals. I was also thinking of the various Rotary and Lions clubs that I now knew from speaking at their meetings—maybe they could help, maybe they knew other clubs that could also help. And my old school . . .

I started a new list and on this one I wrote down everyone I knew. I typed until my eyes grew weary, and then I went back to bed and fell straight asleep.

●

It didn't take long for me to organise to speak at all sorts of different places—clubs, schools, even my nanna's retirement village. Everyone was always really interested and most people supportive. Occasionally people were critical, asking why I supported those in a foreign country instead of supporting Indigenous communities in Australia. It was a good question and I answered honestly—because I would have no idea how to do that.

I set up an extra bank account to start putting donations in. It was a problem though, because I had no option other than to have the account in my name; this always took a lot of explaining every time someone was considering giving money.

As the donations started to roll in and my conversations with Florence became more regular, my passion grew. One day, when I was having a cup of tea with Mum and brainstorming fundraising events with her, she noticed me becoming wild-eyed with excitement. She asked what was going to happen with the scholarship scheme that Jane and I had set up. Jane didn't feel able to find more sponsors, but I knew that I could and I told Mum that ideally the scheme would expand every year, empowering an additional eight girls each year. This meant that next year the scheme would fund sixteen girls into secondary education. At this, Mum asked whether empowering the people of Namwendwa would always be a large part of my life. It was a massive question, but I didn't even flinch before answering.

There was a pause in the conversation then, while Mum and I busied ourselves sipping our tea; I wondered where this series of questions was leading. Finally, when our mugs were empty, Mum revealed her thoughts and suggested that I register my fundraising as an official charity. She said that it would then be easier for me to get donations and other forms of support. I could also open a bank account in the name of the charity.

It sounded like a dramatic thing to do, to set up a charity. Shit, I was just a kid myself—this was possibly way out of my depth. But Mum was right; it would make it easier to gain support. I would no longer have to personally meet every single person before they made a donation.

I rang a long-time family friend, Brad Butler, to ask his opinion and for his advice. I knew that he was involved with Oxfam and he generally seemed to be just an all-round knowledgeable guy. And he didn't disappointment me. Brad told me that there were different types of charity-like organisations. Trust funds, for instance, raised money but then gave it to other organisations to spend. He said that what I was talking about would be a not-for-profit incorporated body. He went on to explain the process for becoming incorporated. For starters, I would need a name for it, plus a governing body and a constitution. He said he would help me if I decided to go ahead.

I always mull over small decisions, like what to eat for dinner, and yet I have a tendency to make big decisions in just a blink. I like to think this is because the big things are so important that you just know what you have to do; and if you don't know, well, that in itself is your answer. This particular decision was no exception, and I immediately told Brad that I would love his help. I said that the organisation would be called 'One Village'.

●

I was in one of my journalism classes for uni, and was twiddling my thumbs and staring at the clock. I must have looked totally out of it because the girl next to me asked whether I was really tired. I sighed and said yes, because that was the easy answer. And I *was* tired—tired of uni.

It was a little amusing that I was already over this course, even though I rarely attended my classes. Each day before I entered the uni grounds, I was the happiest person alive; but then I became brain dead, drifting around the campus like a lost soul. I had to laugh when I realised I was there by choice—I was even paying to be there. In a very warped way

I was paying to be unhappy! It was downright absurd, but still some little voice in my head said it was the right thing to do.

When I arrived back at Sharon's later that day, Nanna was sitting in the lounge room and she was very excited that I was home. She told me that since I had spoken at her retirement village several people had approached her and asked if I would speak at other functions. Brilliant! My networks were growing, but the problem was the times at which people wanted me to speak—I had uni classes that couldn't be missed. Nanna wasn't disappointed and simply said that I had to know my priorities and uni was my main one. Again, I had to laugh; the statement sounded so ridiculous—uni my priority?!

That night was the final straw. I went to see a local high school drama production. I was so excited about being there that I had to use all my will power to restrain myself from jumping up on the stage. I really missed acting. All during my childhood and teen years I had dreamt of being an actress. When I was in Year 11 the lead girl for the Year 12 drama production had fallen sick only two weeks before the opening night. My drama teacher asked if I would take her place, and I was thrilled to accept. We had to rehearse intensely. The play was about a man and woman who initially despised each other, but ended up falling in love. This was how I had met Jack. He played the leading male role. It was a fairytale way to meet.

During Year 11 I attended drama classes three nights a week; I even had an agent. But as the end of Year 12 drew near, I began to doubt myself—*I'm not that talented, hardly anyone gets a break* . . . *blah, blah, blah, excuse, excuse, excuse* . . . The truth was, I had been too scared to even try to make a living out of acting.

I felt the same thing happening to me now—I was only enrolled in uni out of paranoia. Would everyone think I was an idiot if I was not at uni? Would my life ever amount to anything? What would I have to show for myself? Gah, I was so sick of being afraid. I was exhausted with trying to fulfil social expectations. I believed that it was a real privilege to know what made me happy. When I was planning development projects with Andrew, Moses and Florence, or organising my return trip to Uganda for next year, or acting or dancing, my soul and heart came to life. How good did it feel to be alive!

Nanna had said earlier that I needed to know my priorities. My main priority was to be happy—what else was the point of this crazy journey we call life? I had already finished the first semester of my studies, and was about two weeks into the second. If I withdrew from the course now, I would still have a HECS debt for the first semester classes but not the second. So, just like that, I made another snap decision and the next day I withdrew from the course. This was in early August. I could always re-enrol another time if I wanted to.

While I was on a roll of life-altering actions, I decided to take yet another chance—I would tell Tom how I felt about him. Because I still wasn't completely courageous, I called him rather than revealing my feelings in person. As the phone was ringing, I was pacing about my bedroom. What was it with anxiety and pacing?

When he answered, I suddenly felt overwhelmed. In a blubbering ramble I announced that I had feelings for him, and then I hung up. Tom rang me back immediately. I had taken him completely by surprise, but apparently in a really good way. I started smiling when he said that he had feelings for me too and asked if I would like to go on a date. Eagerly I told him about a female musician who was coming to Adelaide and who I really wanted to see. Her name was Holly Throsby and no-one I asked had heard of her. But, amazingly, Tom said that he loved her music and that he had already planned to go to her gig. Now we would go to it together instead.

It was weird. Now that I kept following my heart, everything seemed to be falling into place. It was funny that I had thought that going to uni and doing what society expected of me was swimming with the current, but really I had been swimming against it. As if a higher power wanted to give me further proof that I was on the right track, when I got off the phone from Tom my phone rang again. This time it was a man named Allan Wood, who was a graphic designer and also worked in a printing shop. He was printing newsletters for my old school when an article about me setting up One Village as a charity caught his attention. He read that I was looking for support and was now calling with the offer to donate his time to design a logo for One Village. I couldn't believe my luck and arranged to meet him the following week.

Tom and I had our date. The gig was at a funky little venue called the Grace Emily Hotel and we met there. At first it felt a little strange; I was so used to being around him, but not in this context. When Holly came on the stage everyone sat down on the floor—it was a peaceful vibe. Tom and I were so close that our knees were touching. Her songs were even more beautiful when heard live. I got tingles when she began to sing my favourite song.

As she was singing, Tom took my hand in his. I couldn't have imagined a more perfect moment. Afterwards we shared our first kiss. Tom was completely different from anyone I had ever met and I already adored him.

I was working almost every day in the bakery by now, trying to save money for my return flight to Uganda. Most days it didn't bother me that this work was so undemanding. My mind was always daydreaming anyway, but sometimes I became bored and frustrated.

With Brad's help I drafted a constitution for One Village, but I still needed more members for the governing body. I would be president and Mum vice-president, Brad had offered to be treasurer and my best friend Kaitlyn said she would be the secretary, but I still needed at least two other members.

I met with Allan and we began to work on the logo. It was a really fun process; he would ask me all sorts of questions about colours and different images, trying to find ways that would best portray Namwendwa and the projects. I really liked the idea of orange and green. Orange like the dirt and green for the fertility of the country, but also to portray that One Village worked from the ground up—with needs and projects identified and implemented by the community affected. I also wanted the logo to reflect the idea of coming together to work for a common good, to signify that we are all connected. As I talked, Allan took notes and often he made sketches.

We met a few times and then Allan did some draft logos for me to comment on. I adopted the path of Ugandan honesty, and told Allan everything I liked and disliked about each logo. A few weeks later, he emailed me another design and it was perfect. I went to visit him the next week and expressed my gratitude. To my delight, he said that he had become so interested in One Village that now he wanted to stay involved. I asked him if he wanted to be on the board and he happily accepted.

Then things got even better. He told me that he knew a web designer who might be able to assist me in getting a site up and running. This was how I met Jay Rafferty, who turned out to be an IT guru and an absolute legend. He was only my age but had already started his own web business. His intelligence and drive were inspiring. He not only donated the time he took to design a website for One Village, but also donated the site itself and joined our board.

We now had everything we needed and One Village could register as an incorporated body.

●

I had been speaking to Andrew a lot recently; to my relief, he had taken on responsibility for the scholarship program.

He had been busy collecting letters from the girls and their photos so we could give them to sponsors back here in Australia. The community was thrilled, he said, when he told them that we would expand the program and offer sixteen scholarships next year.

Andrew and Moses also hosted a community meeting to discuss the core needs of the village. An issue that was raised as a primary concern was malnourishment, particularly among children. The community wanted to establish an agricultural program in Namwendwa Primary School. The school had 2½ acres of land that could be used for this. Ideally it would work by introducing agriculture into the curriculum, and then the students would learn to grow the vegetables and fruit for themselves. We would also need to construct a simple building to be used as a kitchen and storage area. Each student would then receive a healthy lunch every day. The program would be low-budget to set up, and then fully sustainable.

I recalled a moment the year before when Andrew had been helping me with the charcoal stove and he had noticed me chopping up a carrot. He had given me an odd look and asked what this funny-shaped orange thing was. I was surprised by his question. I had purchased the carrots from Kamuli, which was only 16 kilometres away, and yet Andrew had never seen a carrot before. I encouraged him to have a taste of it raw and then explained that it could also be cooked. Curious, Andrew took a bite, and then he smiled in delight. 'It's wonderful!' he had exclaimed. When I showed him a capsicum and some green beans, he was equally amazed.

When I first arrived in Uganda I had been blown away by how green and fertile the country was, and I had immediately thought it was a place where no-one should go hungry. As the months passed in Namwendwa, however, I came to realise that there were two issues—the first was not always having enough to eat and the second was not eating the right food. Plenty of vegetables and fruit could grow in Namwendwa, but if people didn't even know that such foods existed or their health benefits, then obviously they wouldn't be growing them. Setting up an agricultural program in the primary school would not only have the long-term benefit of teaching and feeding the students but also hopefully produce a ripple effect when the students carried such knowledge back to their homes.

As well as discussing the possibility of the agricultural program, Andrew and I talked about running a second Health Community Outreach Program and a Disability Awareness Community Outreach Program. Often when I got off the phone, my mind would be buzzing from thinking about the projects we were planning. But discussing these developments was the interesting part; now I had the challenge of raising the funds to turn these possibilities into realities.

I needed to raise the One Village profile, and so I contacted all local media and told them my story. Being young gave me a distinct advantage and seemingly made it all the more newsworthy; newspapers and radio stations took interest in both my experiences and the charity I had set up. I also continued to speak at clubs, schools and even churches. To anyone who would listen, I'd explain how motivated and determined the people of Namwendwa were to improve their situation—they just needed a little help to get things started. I was overwhelmed by the support that people showed, and felt more than ever that we were all coming together as one community, one village.

Most of my days were still spent in the bakery. I had now decided that not only would I return to Uganda in January of the following year, but also that I would later in the year spend some time in South America. While deferring my journalism studies had been an easy decision, I was now missing the Spanish classes that had been part of my course. This way I would learn Spanish the authentic way.

In October I turned 20. I was now officially out of my teens and, to celebrate, I had lunch with Mum, Josh and Sam. Dad was away working somewhere—sometimes I lost track of his whereabouts.

But that night was truly special. Tom picked me up and took me to the beach. The moon shone magnificently bright and the stars appeared to be smiling down at me. The waves swept rhythmically onto the beach, and only the cold sensation of the sand between my toes convinced me this perfect moment was real.

Tom and I sat on the beach. He had brought along his guitar and harmonica. His stunning blue eyes looked at me intently and then he started singing. He had written me a song and it was beautiful—it was called 'My Little Light' and it was about the light that I brought into his life. His singing was so joyful and mesmerising that I knew right then and there that I was in love.

Meantime, the paperwork for One Village's incorporation had been lodged and it continued to consume my life. When I wasn't on the phone to Florence, Andrew or Moses, I was organising fundraisers. Tom and I held a BBQ outside the bakery where I worked. The bakery donated the bread and the butchers next door donated the sausages.

Tom also ran a benefit gig himself. He organised for his band and others to play, and charged a door entry with proceeds to One Village. Tom's best friend, Nick, was like the third musketeer and he did all the artwork for the promotional posters. It was exciting how each of our passions came together to create this special event. Generally, it was also just great to be with someone else who was so interested in One Village and would do anything to support me.

Tom was socially and politically engaged, intelligent and arty. I never told him this, but when I first met him I had found him completely intimidating. Not just because he already seemed to speak fluent Spanish, while I fumbled over *hola,* but because he was so comfortable with himself. He never tried to be anyone or anything other than who he was—it was refreshing.

●

By November I had now saved enough money for my trip and purchased a world ticket. I planned to spend six months in Uganda and then roughly six months in South America.

I was so excited after buying the ticket that I went straight to Tom's to share my good news with him. Tom's face dropped as I told him. Obviously he had known for some time that I planned to leave the following year; but now it was more than a plan, it was real.

I had been so consumed with everything I was going towards that I had forgotten about everything I would be leaving behind. Tom said that he had been thinking about me leaving and had decided that he wanted to come away with me. He said that he couldn't imagine a year without me. He couldn't afford to leave in January, when my flight was booked; but if he worked full-time from now on, he could meet me in Uganda four months into my trip.

This was the first time Tom had mentioned the idea of coming with me and his suggestion at first took me aback. I guess I had just imagined doing the trip on my own, and I also felt funny about the idea of someone making choices just to be with me. Tom was pretty hurt when I stupidly voiced these thoughts.

During the week that followed I began to realise how amazing it would actually be to have him by my side. So finally I told him that I would love for him to come. It would be especially great for him to meet all the people in Namwendwa whom I constantly talked about.

●

The months passed quickly and, before I knew it, it was Christmas. I spent the day with my family, treasuring each moment in the knowledge that in a month's time I would be away again. Josh was especially excited and was racing madly about the house. He was 16 now, but in many ways it seemed that he never grew any older than a child. Often this was a sad thought but, at moments like this when he was so full of joy because we were having croissants for breakfast and because he had presents under a tree, I was able to smile at his everlasting youth.

In the evening I met with Tom. I had put together a treasure chest of gifts for him, just small things that I knew he liked such as sandalwood soap. He gave me a photo album filled with photos of us. He told me to pull each photo out of the album and, when I did so, I discovered that he had written little notes on the back of each photo. 'Memories for while we are apart', he told me.

So far we had spent our time dreaming up the adventures we would have when overseas together, but had spoken little about the four months that we would first have apart. The photo album was a thoughtful gift, but it also made me sad. I still didn't want to think about saying goodbye.

●

At the start of January 2007 One Village was officially launched. My friend Samantha and I had organised the launch party and we hosted it at Tom's mum's cafe. It was normally just a lunchtime cafe but she had kindly offered for us to use it for the evening. We had invited everyone from local politicians to all forms of media, all the people who had supported One Village so far, plus possible sponsors and anyone else we thought might be interested.

Most people invited showed up. Both the local paper and the state-wide paper came and took photographs and ran articles. Even the local politicians made appearances, but then told me off for not speaking until later in the evening. They had other places to be and wanted me to get my speech over with so they could leave. I was a little annoyed that they were telling me what to do and wondered if they would make such comments if I was older or if I was male. I didn't think they were the most important people in the room and so I wanted to wait until those who had actually supported One Village were there. I told the politicians to leave if they needed to.

When I did speak I introduced the Australian One Village Committee and spoke about the people of Namwendwa and the projects we had already initiated. I thanked those who had already shared this passion, and everyone for coming on the night to celebrate everything that was to come. We served wine that had been donated and Tom played acoustic music in the background. It was a great night. Exactly what I had wanted—professional but personal, just like One Village.

When everyone left and we had finished clearing up, Tom and I put all the tables and chairs back in their normal places. Then we sat down together. I was exhausted but content, pleased that everything had gone as planned. Tom seemed quiet, almost agitated. I asked if he was okay, and he confessed that he was a little hurt that I hadn't personally introduced him to everyone on the committee. He had heard me talk about Allan Wood and some of the others so often that he had been really looking forward to meeting them, but hadn't had the chance. At first I felt terrible that I hadn't thought of this, then I felt touched that it was so important to Tom to know the people that were so special to me.

When I went to bed that night, I thought again about what Tom had said and realised that it was so difficult to balance everything. Even with my family, friends and Tom being so interested in One Village, it still felt nearly impossible to find the right way to give each person the attention they needed. One Village was *always* my first priority. Perhaps if it were a selfish endeavour that occupied all my time, it would have been easier for those I loved to say that I wasn't always a good friend, a good daughter, a good sister, a good girlfriend. Yes, I was spending all my time trying to help others; but at the same time, unconsciously, I knew that I had often neglected those who cared for me the most.

I felt like the luckiest person alive, but for the same reason I also felt cursed. There were people I loved on either side of the world and it seemed impossible for me to be there for everyone. It didn't matter where I was or what I was doing, by doing one thing I was in turn always neglecting someone else. This seemed to be the catch 22 of my life.

There were moments when I felt so alive, as though I had the whole world at my feet; but then at other times it felt like the world was on my shoulders. I had become not just empathetic for the people of Namwendwa but for everyone in need, which one way or another was everyone alive.

I decided that I had to focus my thoughts and concentrate only on those closest to me—my family and Tom. I had to think of development only in terms of Namwendwa. This alone was overwhelming—the consideration of anyone else or anything more was too much even to try to comprehend.

The day I left Adelaide to return to Namwendwa came soon enough. My mum, Dad, Josh, Tom and a few friends came to say goodbye to me at the airport. I was going to miss everyone to such an unbelievable degree. My only consolation was that by leaving Australia I was returning to those in Uganda whom I also considered my family and friends.

13

One Village

NAMWENDWA, UGANDA, 29 January 2007

As the plane sweeps down into Entebbe airport, I smile at the sight off the lush jungle below. It is as breathtakingly beautiful as I remember. We land, and it is strange to walk into the tin-shed airport knowing what to expect. I pass quickly through Customs, and am soon back outside in the humidity. It is only early in the morning but still taxi drivers swarm me.

I could take a local bus to Kampala and then onto Jinja, but that would take more hours and effort than I am willing to give. So taxi it is. I speak to the drivers in Lusoga and barter for the best price to get me to Jinja. Lusoga is not the local language in this area but it is similar enough for us to be able to converse. I am slightly proud to surprise the taxi drivers; they did not anticipate that this young white girl would know this place so well.

Once in a taxi, I stare outside and realise immediately that in Australia some of my memories had been romanticised. Now that poverty surrounds me, its familiarity does not ease how confronting I find it. Perhaps that's a good thing.

Along the way, I ask the driver to pull over and I buy a SIM card from a small phone company store. SIM cards are cheap and easy to buy almost anywhere in Uganda. Inside the car I slip the SIM into my phone and text Tom to let him know that I have arrived safely.

Natalie and Lindy, friends from my first trip, are also in Uganda and are staying at a Jinja guesthouse. I decide to go straight there to meet them. Natalie was originally an SPW volunteer from the UK, but in 2005 she fell in love with a Ugandan man and I don't think she ever went home. Or, more accurately, she found herself a new home. She is staying at the guesthouse only temporarily, while she moves places in Jinja.

And Lindy? Well, like myself she too had returned to Australia and I think struggled to slide back into the life she had left behind. She flew back to Uganda only a few days ago, and I think she plans to stay a month or so.

The guesthouse has a high gate and a security guard. Such features are supposed to make me feel safe, but they have the opposite effect—I don't want to believe that such precautions are really necessary.

Natalie and Lindy are excited to see me. As I walk to Lindy's room to dump my bag, I notice a sticker on her door. It reads: 'Are you here as the solution or as part of the problem?' The words stick in my head as I drop my bag and then follow her into the lounge area, where she, Natalie and I gossip away the hours.

I become aware suddenly of the time. It is nearly midday now, and I am eager to get to Namwendwa. I collect my bag, give the girls my new Ugandan phone number and then disappear back out through the high security gates. I am wearing my oversized red backpack. It is a strange shape and sits so high on my back, with its top far above my head, that I am in danger of toppling backwards as I attempt to walk. Of course, I have always known it was uncomfortable but I am desperate to make use of this silly bag that I once thought was so essential for me to purchase.

It is only a five-minute walk from the guesthouse to the main street in Jinja. *Buda-buda* men call out to me but, despite the discomfort of my bag, I want to walk. It's an opportunity to re-adjust to my surroundings. I pass a large metal bin, at least 3 metres wide, and it is overflowing with rubbish. Later it will be set alight, but for now large storks forage through it. The birds look like they belong on top of an old haunted castle.

The storks are not the only hunters in there. Small children also rummage through the scraps. The little clothing that the kids own is as dirty and torn as the rubbish they are searching through. I hate being another person who just walks on by, but what else can I possibly do?

I am surprised when I arrive at the main street and immediately see many white faces. Foreigners are meandering down the street, admiring the souvenirs at shop fronts, popping into internet cafes. I stand a little bewildered, and then realise a child is pulling at my skirt and holding out their other hand for money. I didn't remember Jinja as being like this. I shake my head and say '*Mbe*' (no). The child lets go of my skirt and mopes away.

There are definitely more street children now than there were two years earlier, and more foreigners too. Is it a coincidence? I doubt it. I think of the sticker on Lindy's door . . . Are you here as the solution or part of the problem? I know that good intentions do not always equate to effective and sustainable development, and so I make a mental note to always think about not only how potential projects are identified and implemented but also how they will be monitored and evaluated. These thoughts are a little overwhelming while I'm still in my jet-lag state and now I am feeling uncomfortable and unsure of things.

I leave the main street and walk down to the *matatu* station. I hop straight onto a bus going to Kamuli. While we wait for more passengers, I pull out my iPod. This trip has a whole new soundtrack. No more Missy Higgins—now it is Holly Throsby's soft voice flowing through me.

I feel more relaxed now that I am on the bus, surrounded by locals, with people chatting away. Outside there are people selling everything from plastic hair combs to fried bread and ladies underwear. They crowd around the buses, carrying their goods on sticks that they rest behind the backs of their heads. I nod toward a man selling *chapattis* and he immediately comes to my window. I pack my iPod away, push open the slide window and make my purchase. The man hands me a small sweaty plastic bag, and I leave the window open as I indulge in my snack. The *chapatti* is greasy but delicious in its simplicity. I tear off small bits to eat.

The bus is now crammed with people. There are goats squashed under the seats with their legs tied; there is luggage stacked on the roof; and I'm sure I can hear some chickens squawking, but I can't see them. We rattle on our way. I think that all the drivers here are actually wannabe racing car drivers as it is constant mayhem on the roads. Dirt is now flying in through my open window and getting in my eyes. I push the window shut again. Without the flowing air, the humidity is intense. Sweat gathers between my legs and under my skirt; I feel myself sticking to the vinyl seat. But I'm too distracted to care—my thoughts are in Namwendwa, which is now only a few hours away.

We arrive in Kamuli and I wait by the bus as mattresses and all sorts of random items are lifted off the roof. Somewhere among this assortment is my pack. *Buda-buda* men are already calling out to me, asking where I am going. But I don't answer. I'm still looking for my bag. Finally it is passed down to me; it is more brown than red now. I am amused at how sweaty and dirty I am, yet I haven't even been in this country for 24 hours. Everyone around me looks so clean and, as they would say, 'smart'. Even the women in their full-body *gomesis*, seem to cope with the heat. I look a little ridiculous.

I heave my bag onto my back and approach one of the *buda-buda* men who had earlier called out. It would be cheaper and safer to get a *matatu* to Namwendwa, but it is already getting late in the afternoon and I would likely be waiting for several hours for a *matatu* to leave. The motorbikes are still as dangerous as last time I was here—no helmets, and most of the drivers swerve about like madmen—but I am more impatient than I am sensible, and so I opt for the fast but possibly riskier option. The *buda-buda* man and I quickly agree on a price, and I haul my skirt up and clamber on. There is no way that I am going to try to side-saddle while wearing my enormous top-heavy bag.

We begin to cruise down the dirt road. My bag is strapped onto my back, my arms are wrapped tightly around the *buda-buda* man to stop me falling off backwards, and my skirt is provocatively high. Dirt is flying onto my face and bare legs. This is the sort of moment where I would expect to be feeling seriously uncomfortable, but instead I am deliriously happy. I love the feeling of the wind sailing through my hair—it's exhilarating.

My heart is beating quickly with nervous excitement as we approach Namwendwa. When I see the phone tower beside Florence's home, I ask the *buda-buda* driver to stop. As I am climbing off the bike, Florence is already racing out to the road to meet me.

'Madam Nik!' she exclaims, hugging me even though I still have my bag on. She is crying and tells me that she can't believe that I have really returned. She says that she is so, so happy.

My bag was not the only thing hindering our hug and, as I take a step back from Florence, I realise that she is pregnant. She had not mentioned this news on the phone. I tap her round belly and she laughs. She is expecting her baby any day now. She tells me that her motherly instinct tells her that he is a boy and she is naming him Nicholas, after me. I don't know what to say. I don't want her to feel that she owes me anything or that she needs to show her gratitude. But when I say that it's not necessary to call him after me, she gives me a hurt look, and so I smile and say it's a lovely name.

Now Florence is happy once more, and she tries to take my bag from me. No way am I letting her carry my heavy bag while she is carrying a baby inside her! I take her hand and she guides me up the little dirt path to her home. It feels like déjà vu until I see the infants school. What was once the bamboo classroom has collapsed and is now a heap of rubbish on the ground. As we stand there, she shakes her head and mutters something about the termites.

I tell her that soon a new building will be built there and her school will be stronger than ever. She squeezes my hand. There is a lot we need to talk about, but it is late in the afternoon now and I still want to say hello to Andrew and Moses. I tell Florence that I will be back tomorrow and then I start the 2-kilometre walk to my old home.

The route is as magnificent as ever—orange dirt and overflowing greenery, the colours of One Village. As I walk, children call out to me and many race onto the road and join me. They each want a turn to hold my hand, and I am honoured that they remember me.

When I reach my old home Andrew and Moses are sitting outside waiting. They stand up when they see me, and Moses starts jumping and clapping with joy. I love his child-like mannerisms. I greet them and they are so excited to open the doors for me. Unlike when I first arrived two years ago, this time the house is ready. Andrew and Moses have already cleaned the place out and put in a bed for me, as well as a charcoal stove and basins. I thank them and then ask them where the landlord is so I can pay rent, but they won't allow it. It seems a little strange to be in this same home without Jane, Lillian or Wemusa, but I smile when I recall that in a few months Tom will be living here with me.

After I have put my things inside, the children from the house across the road come and visit me. At first they are shy, but when I lift Victoria into the air, cuddling her and spinning around, the others soon come and join in. Mirimu has grown taller, but still wears the same torn navy blue dress. I can tell that Kisashi is still as moody as ever, but she nods her approval that I have returned and to suggest that she has forgiven me for leaving in the first instance.

I notice Dawoodee by the tree. He still seems unsure—as if he doubts that it is really me. Then I see that he is holding something; I wonder if it his ball, but then I realise it's photographs. I gesture him over and he comes and sits beside me on the wooden chairs out the front. He greets me quietly and then holds out his hands, revealing his treasures. He is holding all the photos and letters that I had posted back to him. He has kept them all. He then confides to me that he didn't really believe I would come back. He asks how long I will stay, and I tell him six months. He nods slowly. We are both thinking the same thing—it's not long enough, it never is.

As we sit together and night creeps in, I think how easily I could live here forever. Yes, I would miss people and I would miss hot showers, but this feels like home. For now, while we are setting things up—registering One Village as a charity in Uganda, opening a bank account, organising how we are going to communicate over the years to come—I know I am of use here. But in the long term I am of more use in Australia, fundraising and telling everyone who will listen about the amazing people of Namwendwa.

It is dark now and Dawoodee returns home for dinner. I'm too tired to cook, so instead I sit on my own and look up at the spectacular night sky. There is the Northern Star, still shining bright. I smile, thinking of everything that has led me back here. In life we don't always follow the path that we had expected—instead we make our own way.

Where this journey will lead is not really clear, but I know that my values will always give me direction. So far there have been many testing moments, times when I questioned myself and everything else too. There have also been amazing achievements, laughter shared and lessons learnt. But the most overwhelming, terrifying and greatest thing of all is to sit here now and realise that this is just the beginning.

This is just the beginning.

Acknowledgements

This book would not have happened without Allen & Unwin, in particular Kathryn Knight and Claire Kingston. I must also specially mention Richard Walsh. I can't thank you enough—for believing that I had a story worth telling and the ability to tell it.

I must next acknowledge my family. Thank you Dad for insisting that I should do that which I love, and Mum for *always* being there when following my heart isn't as easy as I think it should be.

Thank you to both the Ugandan and Australian One Village committees for your continued passion and determination.

Thank you to all the supporters of One Village for sharing this dream and helping turn it into a reality.

And, of course, all of my gratitude to the forever inspiring community of Namwendwa. You have shown me that we can't choose what happens to us, but we can always choose how we react. This book is for you.

About One Village

From the smallest seed grows change.

Our vision is to work in partnership with communities in Eastern Uganda to help them achieve long-term goals that will improve their quality of life.

One Village currently works with the communities of Namwendwa and Butaaya. We believe that effective and lasting development will only come when the community takes ownership and responsibility for projects, and directs the form that they take. From the day One Village began, our projects have been initiated and driven by people passionate about affecting change in their community. One Village's Ugandan volunteers consult with the community and identify development in sectors such as education, agriculture, water and environmental sustainability. Then, the One Village committees in Australia and Uganda unite to find a solution that best meets the needs of the community. A sustainable approach is always at the forefront of the decision-making process.

One Village is comprised entirely of volunteers and in 2011 our administration cost was only 2%.

We are very excited and proud of all that we have achieved so far. In 2011 One Village had sponsored 36 students through their secondary education in Namwendwa, sponsored 39 students with tertiary scholarships in teaching, nursing and technical courses, established vegetable and fruit gardens in Namwendwa and Butaaya primary schools to provide lunch for the students and teachers at the schools, hosted health awareness days every second year in Namwendwa, implemented EcoSAN composting toilets, and helped to restore and furnish Namwendwa Primary School . . . and this is just the beginning! You will have to check out our website for the rest of this story.

To find out more, become involved or make a donation, please visit www.onevillage.org.au.

About the Author

Nikki Lovell is a law student who lives in South Australia. When she's not studying or doing One Village work, she loves to cook, ride her bike, rock climb and travel. She has climbed in Thailand, Vietnam, China and South Africa in the past year. This is her first book.

If you have enjoyed *We Are One Village*, why not try these other books from Allen & Unwin?

Life Without Limits by Nick Vujicic

Life Without Limits is the story of gutsy Nick Vujicic, an amazing 28-year-old Aussie born without arms or legs, who is now an internationally successful inspirational speaker. Packed full of wisdom, testimonials of his faith and laugh-out-loud humour, Nick tells of life in his 'Chesty Bond' body, his visit to Africa at the age of 20 where he gave away $20 000 of his life savings to the poor, and raised another $20 000 for them on the side, and how he learned to surf, skateboard, dive and more.

Noting that 'perfection isn't always perfect' and that 'brokenness can be a good thing', Nick shows how he learned to accept what he could not control and focus instead on what he could. He encourages everyone to find their life's purpose and, whatever their obstacles, go for it. He's already appeared in an acclaimed short film doing his own stunts, and his zest for life is unbelievably infectious.

Angel in the Rubble by Genelle Guzman-McMillan

'I interviewed Genelle Guzman just after the world changed on September 11, 2001. I wondered how what she went through would affect her life in the years to come. In this eloquent and poignant book, I ended up reassured and inspired. And not just about Genelle, but about humanity. Even though we know Genelle was the "last survivor", the detail in this book is intricate and tense; as you read each word it makes you angry, sorrowful and incredulous all over again. This isn't just Genelle's incredible story . . . this is a story we will never forget.'—Gary Tuchman, CNN national correspondent

Sometimes terrible things happen . . .

On 11 September 2001 Genelle starts her working day like any other: throwing on her high heels, dashing off to work on the 64th floor of the northern Twin Tower of the World Trade Center, organising coffee for workmates and settling down to her work. Then they hear a loud bang. The floor shakes, but nothing dramatic seems to have happened.

Clouds of paper start to float past the window. Some time later Genelle and her co-workers discover a plane has slammed into their building. They're advised to remain where they are, which they do. Eventually they take matters into their own hands and begin to make their way down the endless flights of now empty stairs. They are so near their goal when the building begins to sway and the tower collapses on Genelle. She finds herself alone and unable to move in the dust and the darkness.

This riveting story brings to life Genelle's 27-hour ordeal and rescue from under the debris of the 9/11 World Trade Center wreckage. Genelle, the last survivor to be pulled from Ground Zero, shares her miraculous experiences during those 27 long hours, and the immense richness of her life beyond it.

The remarkable true story of the day that changed Genelle Guzman-McMillan's life.

The Happiest Refugee by Anh Do

Anh Do nearly didn't make it to Australia. His entire family came close to losing their lives on the sea as they escaped from war-torn Vietnam in an overcrowded boat. But nothing—not murderous pirates, nor the imminent threat of death by hunger, disease or dehydration as they drifted for days—could quench their desire to make a better life in a country where freedom existed.

Life in Australia was hard, an endless succession of back-breaking work, crowded rooms, ruthless landlords and make-do everything. But there was a loving extended family, and always friends and play and something to laugh about for Anh, his brother Khoa and their sister Tram. Things got harder when their father left home when Anh was thirteen—they felt his loss very deeply and their mother struggled to support the family on her own.

His mother's sacrifice was an inspiration to Anh and he worked hard during his teenage years to help her make ends meet, also managing to graduate high school and then university. Another inspiration was the comedian Anh met when he was about to sign on for a 60-hour-a-week corporate job. Anh asked how many hours he worked. 'Four,' the answer came back, and that was it—Anh was going to be a comedian!

The Happiest Refugee tells the incredible, uplifting and inspiring life story of one of our favourite personalities. Tragedy, humour, heartache and unswerving determination—a big life with big dreams. Anh's story will move and amuse all who read it.

Saving Private Sarbi by Sandra Lee

Powerful, dramatic and heartwarming, this is the true story of Sarbi, the scruffy black Labrador-cross trained by the Australian Army as an explosives detection dog for the most dangerous combat mission imaginable.

Thirteen months after Australia's most famous canine warrior went missing in action following a historic battle between the elite SAS and the Taliban in Afghanistan in 2008, she was found by an American Special Forces officer patrolling a village in a region known to be a Taliban stronghold. Against all odds, Sarbi had survived her injuries, the enemy's weapons, a bitter winter, one brutal summer and the harsh unforgiving landscape, on her own. She was the miracle dog of Tarin Kot.

Sarbi's story, and those of the other brave Australian Army dogs in Afghanistan, will resonate with anyone who has known the unconditional love of man's best friend and understands the rewards of unbidden loyalty, trust and devotion. It will appeal to all those who appreciate the selflessness of serving your country and the inherent dangers of putting your life on the line for others in a war zone. And it will strike a chord with anyone who has experienced the magical connection with a dog.

Tamil Tigress by Niromi de Soyza

Two days before Christmas in 1987, at the age of 17, Niromi de Soyza found herself in an ambush as part of a small platoon of militant Tamil Tigers fighting government forces in the bloody civil war that was to engulf Sri Lanka for decades. With her was her lifelong friend, Ajanthi, also aged 17. Leaving behind them their shocked middle-class families, the teenagers had become part of the Tamil Tigers' first female contingent.

Equipped with little more than a rifle and a cyanide capsule, Niromi's group managed to survive on their wits in the jungle, facing not only the perils of war but starvation, illness and growing internal tensions among the militant Tigers. And then events erupted in ways that she could no longer bear.

How was it that this well-educated, mixed-race, middle-class girl from a respectable family came to be fighting with the Tamil Tigers? Today she lives in Sydney with her husband and children; but Niromi de Soyza is not your ordinary woman, and this is her compelling story.

Out of the Blue by Joanna Fincham

When Joanna Fincham appeared on a popular reality TV program looking for love in 2008, little did the viewers know that Jo had been suffering from depression all her life.

Jo, it seemed, was a vivacious city girl looking for love with a handsome farmer. On screen she appeared bubbly, warm and happy, but in reality she had struggled with depression and bulimia for many years, both illnesses bringing their own difficulties and experiences.

Despite her struggles, Jo went on to win the show and find love with Farmer Rob. In a fairytale ending Jo moved to the countryside and left her city life behind her.

Now living in South Australia on their farm, Rob and Jo are married with a gorgeous baby daughter. This is the story of how Jo tackled her demons, found love and created a new, healthy, happy life free from depression. It's a story of how love really can conquer all and how life on the land can heal and nurture you.

Inspiring, warm and fiercely honest, this is a wonderful personal account of overcoming adversity and making the most of life.